The KARATE-DO
Teachings of Masami Tsuruoka

Andrew W. Bowerbank

MORRIS
MARKETING AND MEDIA SERVICES
Toronto, Ontario, Canada

Disclaimer: The author, publisher, and/or any contributors to this book are NOT RESPONSIBLE in any manner whatsoever for any injury that may result from practising the techniques and/or following the instructions given within. Since the physical activities described herein may be too strenuous in nature for some readers to engage in safely, it is essential that a physician be consulted prior to training.

Published by Morris Marketing
and Media Services Inc. of Toronto, Ontario, Canada

ISBN 0-9682528-0-X

Copyright© 1997 by Morris Marketing and Media Sevices Inc.
All rights reserved

Bound and printed in Canada

I met Tsuruoka *Sensei* more than 30 years ago and have come to know him as a dedicated master of *karate-do*. A man who not only knows how to effectively develop and maximize a student's technical skills, but also stands to represent personal commitment and achievement for all to follow. His exemplary character is a light for every *karate-ka*, both beginner and advanced.

The Spirit of Karate-do: Teachings of Masami Tsuruoka is an introductory collection of over half a century of experience. Having this masterpiece on one's bookshelf will prove to be an enriching and informative addition.

JKA
Shotokan

Stan Schmidt
Chief Instructor
South African JKA Karate Association

I first heard of *Sensei* Masami Tsuruoka over forty years ago while I was a resident in Japan. I lived in Beppu City, located on Kyushu, the southern-most main island of Japan. Tsuruoka *Sensei* lived on the western side of the island near the city of Kumamoto. His reputation as an excellent technician and a fierce fighter were legendary all over the island.

No one who sparred with him, even in a friendly bout, ever wanted to repeat the experience. I left Japan and returned to the U.S. in 1954. A decade passed before I had the opportunity to meet this marvelous man in Toronto, Canada, during the summer of 1963. When I was introduced to him, I found it hard to believe that this soft-spoken, one hundred and twenty-five pound gentleman standing before me dressed in a business suit, was the fierce Masami Tsuruoka I had heard about while living in Beppu. A class was scheduled for that evening. We traveled to his *dojo* where he donned his *karate-gi*; it was then that I realized he was indeed the legend I had heard about.

A complete transformation had taken place. His demeanor had changed. Standing before me was *Sensei* Masami Tsuruoka, the father of Canadian karate, outstanding student of Dr. Tsuyoshi Chitose and former terror of Kyushu, Japan. As he walked upon the training floor his presence could be felt throughout the entire dojo. Here was indeed a man of *budo*, a modern warrior. I have trained under the guidance of Tsuruoka *Sensei* for thirty years. Even after this amount of time, he continually amazes me with his technical skill and unlimited knowledge of karate technique, *kata*, *kumite* and history.

After training under Tsuruoka *Sensei* for many years I requested that he write a karate instructional book. "I am not ready to write a book", he replied. "Perhaps someday I will write a book."

For decades I waited patiently. Now my request has been fulfilled. It is not often a "living legend" authors a book. This is one of those unique times. I highly recommend this book to everyone who has donned a *karate-gi* and also to those who wish they had.

William J. Dometrich
Founder/Chief Instructor

United States
Chito-kai

Tsuruoka Karate has a long history in Canada, indeed within the world of karate. The unique theories and techniques developed and evolved by Tsuruoka *Sensei* reflect his own humanity and charisma.

People and karate cannot exist separately from society. I feel the spirit of tranquility is achieved in one of two ways: one either escapes into a world of ideas, or one gathers together like-minded individuals and challenges the world to change. The success of Tsuruoka Karate lies in the integration of these two approaches and leads *karate-ka* into a most appealing world.

The innovative foundations of Tsuruoka *budo* are, at last, revealed for the first time in this book. *Karate-ka* from all styles, novice or advanced students, will find this fascinating and compelling reading.

Kazumi Tabata
President
American University Karate-do Federation

TABLE OF CONTENTS

ACKNOWLEGMENTS / 8
WORDS FROM O-SENSEI / 9
PREFACE / 10

Chapter 1 **Karate-do, A Historical Overview / 13**

Chapter 2 **Kihon Waza / 19**
Ibuki / 22
Tsuruoka *Ibuki* / 23
Messen / 25
Atemi / 27
Kime / 28
Zanshin / 29

Chapter 3 **Catagories of *Kihon Waza* / 33**
Uke Waza / 39
Keri Waza / 41
Ate Waza / 46
Kihon-Dachi / 48
Kihon-Dachi & *Zanshin* / 55
Kumite-Dachi / 56
Tsuruoka Hip Thrust / 57
Hip Rotation / 58
Hip Vibration / 59

Chapter 4 **Tsuruoka *Kihon* Principles / 61**
Hip-Lock Principle / 62
Tight-Release Principle / 65
Extension Principle / 68
Kihon Waza Overview / 71

Chapter 5 **Kata and Kumite / 77**
Kata: Purpose and Practice / 78
History of *Kata* / 80
Tsuruoka Practical-Application *Kata* / 81
Kata and Personal Growth / 84
Kumite: Purpose and Practice / 88
Maai / 91

Chapter 6 **Catagories of *Kumite* / 95**
Gohon- & *Sanbon-Kumite* / 96
Kihon Ippon Kumite / 98
Tsuruoka *Kihon Kumite* / 101
Jiyu Ippon-Kumite / 102
Jiyu Kumite and Sport Karate *Kumite* / 103

Chapter 7 **Principles of Timing / 109**
Go-No-Sen / 111
Sen-No-Sen / 112
Sen / 113

Chapter 8 **The Spirit of Karate-do / 117**
The Karate *Dojo* / 118
A Way of Life / 120

Chapter 9 **Tsuruoka Karate-do / 125**

Chapter 10 **Sketches in Time / 141**
Moving a Mountain / 143
Leap of Faith / 147

Chapter 11 **Words of Encouragement / 153**

Some Remarks for Aspiring *Sensei* / 156

NOTES / 156

GLOSSARY / 160

BIBLIOGRAPHY / 164

ACKNOWLEDGMENTS

This book would not have been possible if not for the untiring efforts of the staff involved in its assembly. Thank you to: Al Rodin for the superb illustrations. Rod Morris for his positive support and advice. Ted Yoshioka for taking time out of his demanding schedule. Martin Hung, David Tsuruoka and John Charry for patience during photography. Linda Mason and Mike Spence for proofreading. Fortunato Aglialoro for design assistance. Craig Kodama for computer set up assistance. Yun Bowerbank for keeping the author's sanity in check.

Special thanks to *O-Sensei* Masami Tsuruoka. Your discipline, drive and ability are an inspiration to us all.

Author
Andrew Bowerbank

Research Advisor
Masami Tsuruoka

Editor
Ted Yoshioka

Illustrator
Al Rodin

Photographer
Andrew Bowerbank
Various Submissions

Book Layout
Andrew Bowerbank
Fortunato Aglialoro

Cover Design
Andrew Bowerbank

Maps & Diagrams
Andrew Bowerbank

Publisher
Rod Morris,
Morris Marketing and
Media Services Inc.

There was an expression commonly used in old Japan that should be re-introduced to modern society, and especially into the world of traditional martial arts: *Giri to ninjō* (obligation and humanity). It carries a powerful message with a lot of responsibility.

Today, martial artists talk about loyalty and respect, but seemingly only act on it if the outcome has positive repercussions. *Giri to ninjō* is a statement that encompasses all concepts of loyalty, dedication, respect, etc., through enforcing a sense of obligation. This obligation (*giri*) becomes a binding ideal dedicated to the betterment of humanity (*ninjō*), whatever the cost to the individual.

Teachers are proud when a student does well under his/her tutelage, but a student that is struggling can be left in the shadows. *Giri to ninjō* forces the teacher to work just as hard if not harder to improve the abilities of the struggling student (*giri*). If this student is allowed to fall behind, the family and friends (*ninjō*) of this student might suffer from the effects of that student's failure.

The *bushido* code that defined the conduct of Japan's samurai class was bound by the concept of *giri to ninjō*. Obligation and commitment to the lord of the clan (*Daimyō*) took precedence over all other concerns, even the concerns of the samurai's own life and personal family. *Giri to ninjō* ensured a samurai would willingly sacrifice his life for the protection or security of the *Daimyō* and his cause.

Unfortunately, in our society *giri* has become a hollow concept. Without a sense of commitment to the safety of others and to the leader who provides direction, all preceding structure and security falls apart. *Giri to ninjō* is a living cycle that must not be interupted.

A true *sensei* is bound by *giri to ninjō*, thus committing totally to the positive development of his/her students. Students are subsequently bound by *giri to ninjō*, offering themselves completely, in return for the knowledge and skill transmitted by the *sensei*. This relationship should be considered a commitment for life.

Masami Tsuruoka

PREFACE

This book is a heartfelt tribute to Masami Tsuruoka, the father of Canadian karate. It begins with a brief historical introduction to karate-do and continues with an exploration of traditional karate-do concepts. A closer examination of Mr. Tsuruoka's own key teaching principles is presented, and the text concludes with a personal look at the man himself.

This work is not meant to be an instructional document alone but is intended to complement one's current training and perhaps help explore new or different avenues of comprehending and appreciating karate-do theory and application. For students currently training in Tsuruoka karate, these pages organize important references to help keep training on track.

Except for names, places and those few words that can now be found in English dictionaries (samurai, karate, etc.), Japanese words appear in italics throughout the text. These are generally accompanied by an English interpretation in parentheses the first time they appear, but are subsequently left to stand on their own. Readers wishing to review these terms can consult the glossary at the back of this book. Japanese names are written with the person's given name first and family name last.

Out of their deep respect for his character and accomplishments, Mr. Tsuruoka's students have directly addressed and referred to him as *O-Sensei*

O-Sensei and author, 1993.

for some years now. This form of address appears in the text for the most part, although there may be a few exceptions due to style or clarity considerations. *O-Sensei's* honorific title has been respectfully omitted from parts of Chapters 9 and 10 in order to enhance the historical sense of personal discovery and the lifelong development of his art.

The author would like to express his appreciation and gratitude for all the inspiration and encouragement he has received from *O-Sensei* over the years, both on and off the dojo floor. He would also like to thank his fellow *karate-ka* - too numerous to mention individually - for their continued support in the course of daily training, for their selfless contribution to the construction of the *Tsuruoka Canadian Budokai Hombu Dojo* in Toronto and for their feedback and encouragement during the researching and writing of this book.

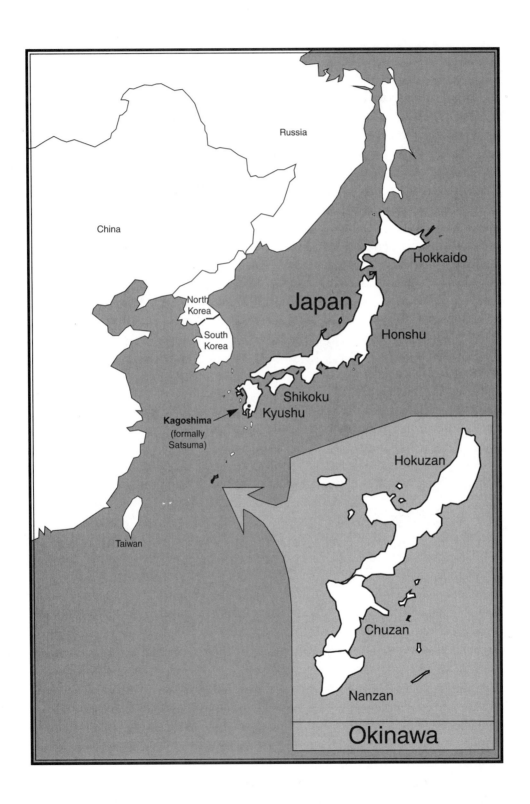

Karate-do: A Historical Overview

空手道の由来

1

A traditional samurai home preserved in Kagoshima (formally Satsuma), Japan.

Karate was developed in Okinawa in response to forcible occupation by samurai from the Satsuma clan of Kyushu. Invaded in 1609, the local inhabitants were forbidden the possession of not only weapons, but any objects made of metal. Under a series of Japanese rulers, the Okinawans were even obliged to check out farming tools each day and bring them back before sundown.[1]

Having a strong sense of pride and determination, Okinawans began to look for means other than traditional weapons to reestablish their independence and rid themselves of their "Japanese burden". They eventually developed various self-defense systems which used farming implements *(kobudo)* and/or bare hands and feet (karate).

The actual events leading to the point where karate became a viable defense option are historically unclear. The local precursor to karate - *tode* ("China hand") - is considered to have been a blend of indigenous techniques with some Chinese influence. The most common theory is that while closed-fist striking was very likely native to Okinawa, the major concepts of stances and open-hand techniques came from China by way of *ch'aun fa* (kung fu), with kicking techniques imported from Cambodia and Laos.[2]

The Okinawans analyzed imported fighting principles and adapted them to their political, sociological and military needs, keeping only those techniques that would help them defend against the occupying force. Karate techniques had to be powerful, fast and devastating. Some say that today's board-breaking demonstrations reflect the historical need to smash through samurai armor and inflict damage to the body behind it.

In the event of an attack, an unarmed Okinawan would have had but one chance to stop his opponent. If the samurai had been allowed a second swing with his sword, the defender would have surely perished. This meant the latter would have had to react with incredible ferocity and spirit, totally committing to the defending technique in order to remain alive. From this mentality came the doctrine which many traditional karate styles still live by, *ikken hissatsu* (one deadly strike).

A modern-day samurai in Kyoto, Japan.

As history has shown in all cultures, military control eventually gives way to civilian rule. Japan gave up its feudal ways with the Meiji Restoration, under which a constitutional

Two examples of traditional kobudo weapons. Left: Sai (truncheon). Right: Nunchaku(rice flail).

monarchy was established in 1868. This opened the way for several significant developments: most of the samurai became civilians and a law decreed in 1876 forbade all but the remaining official military to wear swords. Japan withdrew its occupying force from Okinawa, eliminating the need for karate as a personal system of defense. Across Japan, feudal *bujutsu* (martial "fighting arts") underwent refinement and developed into modern *budo* (martial "ways") - the former had focused on actual combat techniques, but the latter became concerned primarily with self-development through physical training. Schools began to open everywhere to teach these new methods of physical exercise and mental discipline.

Okinawa introduced *karate-do* in its own school system shortly after the turn of the century. At the request of the Japanese Ministry of Education, a young Okinawan schoolteacher by the name of Gichin Funakoshi presented *karate-do* to a large Japanese assembly in Tokyo in 1922. The demonstration was so successful that the government not only permitted *karate-do* to be introduced to the general Japanese population, but several major universities actively incorporated it into their curriculum.

Left: *"Bo" (6 foot staff) instruction at camp kami-kaze, north of Toronto.*

Opposite page: *Two modern-day samurai test their kendo skills in Kagoshima, Japan.*

Overleaf: *Tsuruoka Sensei demonstrates empi (elbow strike).*

Kihon Waza

Ted Jungblut practises the linear focus prevalent in a strong shotokan reverse punch.

Having looked at some of the major points in *karate-do*'s historical development, one begins to understand the reasoning behind the constant use of dynamic *kihon waza* (basic techniques). Since karate was intended for self-preservation against a better-armed opponent, it was necessary to inflict the greatest amount of damage and end a conflict quickly. Powerful linear techniques were developed to achieve this.

The early years of training (*kyu* levels) for a Tsuruoka *karate-ka* (student) are thus based on linear motion and the powerful execution of technique. Some circular motion is introduced, but this is kept to a minimum until a later stage of training (*dan* levels).

Circular techniques tend to be somewhat easier or more natural to apply through the subconscious understanding of centripetal force.[1] A fist moving in a circular motion picks up speed and power as it travels away from the central axis, as can be observed in a basic western boxing punch. This kind of punch usually produces the following effects: surface damage is extensive (bruising, skin lacerations, swelling) while internal damage is minimized (organs and large bones are generally unaffected). These two considerations make circular techniques preferable for contact sports such as boxing and kick-boxing: short-term physical trauma helps determine a match's outcome, but long-term injuries and internal damage are significantly reduced.

Linear impact, on the other hand, causes minimal surface damage and extensive internal damage. The image of a karate strike is similar to that of a competitive high diver entering the water without causing any splashes on the surface of the water. If the dive is performed correctly the diver will enter the water and penetrate deeply, leaving only a minor ripple at the surface.

The difficulty for *karate-ka* is the complex order of operations that must be practised before an effective linear strike can be applied (see tight-release principle in Chapter 4). Unfortunately, correct linear techniques cannot rely on any natural or subconscious sense of motion. This means the linear process must be a learned action, which can take many years to apply correctly as an instantaneous or subconscious response to an attack.

Basic *karate-do* techniques can be placed into one of three categories: blocking, striking and kicking. All of these require strong *kihon-dachi* (basic stances) for powerful application. Each category involves a different physical emphasis for achieving proper form and execution, with variations in application depending on intent, kinetics and body mass.

Factors common to all categories of *waza* (technique) are the constant principles of *zanshin* (awareness), *kime* (decisive focus), *messen* (eye direction) and *atemi* (correct strike on target). *Ibuki* (breathing) works with these four principles to help develop strong basics in all styles of *karate-do*. All of these factors will be discussed before looking at categories of *kihon waza* in order to explore the central connection among all *karate-do* applications.

David Tsuruoka applying zanshin to the shotokan kata - kanku sho.

Ibuki

The two phases of *ibuki* can be understood by observing day-to-day human exertion. The first phase, breathing in, draws air into the lungs and supplies oxygen to the blood. This phase is generally used as preparation before exertion. Effort is not applied at this point; instead, one tends to pause and gather strength and concentration for the imminent use of force. The second phase, exhaling carbon dioxide, then commences: muscles contract, limbs move and force is applied. The lungs then take in air again in preparation for the next task at hand.

Untrained individuals only fully utilize the top sixty per cent of their lungs when going through these phases subconsciously. Athletes, on the other hand, train to control their breathing and utilize the top and bottom portions of their lungs equally. In addition, endurance athletes learn to conserve energy by breathing in rhythm with their actions, while

Cross-training at the Hombu Dojo.

strength athletes, such as sprinters and power lifters, learn to force carbon dioxide out of the lungs in powerful bursts for maximum results.

Modern martial arts, with a strong focus on the sport aspect of their training, generally utilize the procedures and training methods used by sport disciplines such as those mentioned above. Traditional martial arts systems with little or no sport involvement use different *ibuki* exercises to increase speed, stability, balance, composure and focus. The *kiai* (energy shout) in *karate-do* helps integrate and focus these factors at the point where the greatest application of energy is needed.

Tsuruoka *Ibuki*

Many martial artists practise continuously breathing out from the beginning of a technique to the point of *kime*. O-Sensei believes this form of *ibuki* requires too much applied effort which could be saved for a later time. A *karate-ka* must be able to relax and achieve the composure needed to respond instantaneously in any given situation without excess, jerky body motion. Thanks to gravity and body mass, exhaling is a very natural and simple task. However, O-Sensei feels inhaling should be constantly practised as it

In this series, O-Sensei demonstrates ibuki to George Taylor. Top: Breathe in slightly at start. Middle: Force air out from lower abdomen. Bottom: Close off breath for strong kime.

Working hard to apply correct ibuki.

is difficult to master, especially in stressful situations.

The first three-quarters of a *tsuki* (punch) should be dedicated to speed. Any use of power at this stage restricts quick movement by contracting muscles unnecessarily, including those muscles required to force air out of the lungs. Needless contraction at the beginning of the punch causes the shoulder to roll up and forward, interfering with trajectory (see tight-release principle in Chapter 4).

O-Sensei has developed a method of *ibuki* which concentrates on refining and improving the benefits of inhaling air into the lungs. This method is somewhat different from those used in other karate styles: Tsuruoka *karate-ka* breathe *in* for the first three-quarters of a punch. This allows the punch to travel quickly and evenly, eliminating any projection of technique for one's partner to see.

It should be noted at this point that the breath in is controlled, calm and drawn into the lower abdomen only. The chest area must remain relaxed. The breath out is only expelled in the last quarter of the technique and should be sharp and quick, finishing with strong *kime*. Beginners are told to mouth the word "hut" at this point in order to close off the breath. This helps achieve strong *kime* and allows the lungs to hold onto some air in case a second quick surge of energy is called for, as in the application of a combination technique.

After *kime* has been applied and the breath has been closed off, *zanshin* is then relied on to finish off the technique: the remaining breath is slowly and quietly exhaled from the lower abdomen. Energy thus continues to flow out from the end of a technique, keeping the *karate-ka* stable in stance, i.e., balanced with a lower center of gravity, rooted to the ground for strength and support (see extension principle in Chapter 4).

Tsuruoka *ibuki* requires a lot of practice before it can be applied with confidence and subconscious timing. It may well be one of *O-Sensei's* most complex technical concepts. *Messen, atemi, kime* and *zanshin* work in harmony with *ibuki* but are not style-specific. These four constant principles - common to every *karate-do* technique - are generically taught throughout all traditional styles of *karate-do*.

Messen

Messen would be the first constant principle to apply in the practice of *kihon* (basics), *kata* (prearranged forms) and *kumite* (sparring). A *karate-ka* must always have visual contact with his/her partner before any technique can be applied. Initiating techniques based only on touch, anticipated movement or sounds such as an instructor's count would be disorienting. Visual contact allows the mind to instantly analyze situations and make split-second decisions.

The application of *messen* to *kihon waza* is crucial to establishing balance and projecting intensity. Before any technique can be initiated, *messen* must lead rotation of the head in the direction of intent. This allows the inner ear enough time to establish balance and composure. Without *messen*, techniques would be applied by a subconscious "estimated guess" learned over time through the repetition of techniques. In a confrontational situation, however, this estimated guess would not ensure personal safety and control over an aggressor. Students must learn to apply *messen* in the *dojo* (training hall) at all times so that "observation before motion" becomes an immediate subconscious response in defensive circumstances.

Applying correct messen. Top: Applied too late after striking the target. Contact from attacker is imminent. Bottom: Correct aplication allows time to control attacker.

Atemi

Atemi is the second constant principle applied to a technique and requires concentration and common sense to apply properly. The first consideration is to select the best technique for contact with a given target. It would not make sense to use *jodan mawashi-geri* (high roundhouse kick) in close-range fighting or a grappling situation. *Karate-ka* must always apply techniques that attain the traditional goal of *ikken-hissatsu*.

The next consideration is to apply the best technique with proper form. Performing *yoko-geri-kekomi* (side thrust kick) with the toes of the kicking foot pointing up and the heel of the supporting leg off the ground could result in the kicker's toes being broken. Contact must be made with the correct part of the attacking limb and the technique must be supported with correct posture to be effective. In another example, many *karate-ka* find it difficult and frustrating to apply *uchi-uke* (inside middle block) against an attack if the blocking hand leads the technique. *Uchi-uke* becomes very useful, however, if practised properly with the shoulders down and the elbow leading the block. The necessity for proper form illustrates the need to constantly practise and perfect all basic techniques.

The final consideration is to apply the best technique with the correct form exactly on target. Many *kihon waza* can be delivered to different areas on an opponent's body with adequate effect. However, each technique has actually been designed to strike a specific target and must be applied accord-

O-Sensei utilizes correct atemi to win an exchange. The reverse punch is off target, while the jab would have produced devistating results if O-Sensei's intent was to make contact.

ingly to achieve optimum results. Throwing *kizami-zuki* (jab) to the lower abdomen would only present the attacker's face as a prime target for a counter technique - this strike would be better directed at an opponent's head, as it was originally intended to do.

Kime

Kime is the third constant principle that *karate-ka* need to bear in mind. This occurs in the last quarter of a technique, where all the necessary muscles in the body contract to create a solid wall for support. By solidifying the body at the point of impact, the immovable resistance of the earth is transferred through the technique to the opponent, enhancing the effect of the strike, kick or block. This is also the moment that a *kiai* is often expelled to focus power and determination for maximum results.

Contracting muscles to create *kime* does not mean that proper posture and composure are sacrificed. It is possible to overdo muscle contraction to the point where constriction results. This feeling of constriction is very detrimental to posture, form, composure and reaction time. Applying *kime* only at the very last moment of the technique helps establish correct posture and form, and also eliminates constriction (see *ibuki* section above).

Brad Jones applies strong kime to a well-excecuted high side thrust kick.

Physical contraction alone at this point is not enough for complete *kime*. A *karate-ka* must also learn that *kime* incorporates a psychological factor, which is just as necessary as the physical component. As the muscles of the body contract, the mind should concentrate on the single technique at hand to produce a powerful but coordinated effort.

Zanshin

Zanshin can be a very elusive goal for a *karate-ka* to attain consistently. The ability to keep one's intent focused on a single objective for more than a few moments can be a very demanding and tiring process. North American educational researchers have found the average attention span of a university student to be approximately twenty-five to thirty minutes when watching a course lecture from a static position with no outside distractions.[2] An average karate class can run from one hour to three hours in length, with many distractions to interfere with concentration.

A kyu belt practises zanshin.

Zanshin proves to be more than just the ability to stay focused on a given task, but this basic understanding provides a good foundation on which to build. There are two moments where *zanshin* is applied to the exchange of techniques. The first is before a technique is initiated. This is where a *karate-ka*

Tsuruoka Sensei demonstrates stone / brick breaking in this early 1960s photo. Atemi, messen, zanshin, kime and ibuki work together at one decisive moment.

must feel in tune with his/her partner's state of mind, rhythm, and tension level, able to react instantaneously and correctly to any sudden movement. This awareness must come from the *tanden* - the point one to two inches below the navel, then two inches in - where it is believed *ki* (energy) originates. Strong *zanshin* can also help keep an attacker at bay by projecting determination and a formidable spirit, creating an invisible but intimidating wall of defense.

The second moment *zanshin* is applied is immediately after a technique has been completed. This helps strengthen stability, balance and extension of force. It also produces composure and determination, allowing a *karate-ka* to respond immediately to any possible counter techniques.

Zanshin can be considered a means of linking *kihon waza* together to create a strong, continuous defensive strategy. When *karate-ka* face each other in *kumite*, there should never be a constant exchange or barrage of techniques. Extended moments exist where neither partner will mount an attack. This is not because the protagonists need to rest between exchanges; instead, they need time to analyze defensive positioning before initiating the best possible attack. The attacker projects *zanshin* at this point to increase determination and psychological intimidation for the greatest chance of penetrating a presented defense. The defender uses *zanshin* to improve posture and eliminate possible target zones. If both sides have equally strong *zanshin*, then *kumite* could result in a stalemate, with neither side able to attack. If one side detects *suki* - a lapse or weakness in *zanshin* - in the other, he/she will be able to initiate an effective attack.

Although *zanshin* is not a physical technique, it is one of *karate-do*'s crucial strategic principles. Maintaining strong *zanshin* outside the *dojo* projects confidence and a strong will which can be used to settle disagreements or even deter aggression, repelling potential assailants before any physical attack can occur.

Categories of Kihon Waza

3

基本的業の部類

This chapter explores the purely physical aspects of *karate-do* techniques. Although application and strategic intent are generic to all systems, each style of *karate-do* has its own means of preparing, presenting and executing its *kihon waza*, with different emphasis on each technique. For example, some systems rely on or stress strong dynamic *gyaku-zuki* (reverse punch) and *yoko-geri* (side kick); others emphasize the sharp whipping actions of *uraken* (back fist) and *mae-geri* (front kick).

Reflecting technical differences among the different styles, some *karate-ka* might contend that one style is nothing like the other. They may even go so far as to state that one certain style is better than another. This line of contention would be short-sighted and contrary to the spirit in which *karate-do* was developed. Styles must inevitably share many similarities as they all come from the same prime origin in Okinawa. Their common use of the term *karate-do* defines a basic martial theory which connects them all through similar lines of development and related concepts.

To reiterate, one style of *karate-do* is not better than any other. Different styles develop based on a number of factors, two of which will be explored here. The first factor is body type, classified by modern science into three general categories:

A beginner works to improve his basic techniques.

Ectomorph
- light bones, very little fat
- linear appearance with frail and delicate bone structure
- small, narrow chest and a shorter trunk relative to the arms and legs

Endomorph
- heavy bone structure and pads of soft, rounded flesh
- trunk roughly the same girth from the shoulders to the hips
- weight concentrated around the middle of the body
- little bone and muscle definition
- bones and joints relatively small compared to body size

Mesomorph
- heavy bone structure, little fat, well-muscled
- wide shoulders, narrowing to slender hips
- good muscle definition, particularly in arms, chest and back

Ectomorph.

Endomorph.

Mesomorph.

Given these physical differences, it would not be practical to teach an endomorph the same concepts and techniques as a mesomorph and expect the same results. Various styles of *karate-do* were therefore developed over time to enhance the strongest abilities of each body type. For example, modern *shotokan* would best suit the athletic abilities of the mesomorph, *goju-ryu* would develop the powerful attributes of the endomorph and *wado-ryu* could enhance the lightning-quick reflexes of the ectomorph. There are also many styles, such as *chito-ryu,* which seem to combine technical emphasis, just as nature has formed body types which appear in combined classifications, for example, ecto-endomorph. Of course, readers should not assume that people of different body types should be automatically locked into learning *karate-do* styles that would only be best for their particular physical makeup. Every style contains a wealth of information that will dramatically benefit anyone wishing to learn.

Tsuruoka Students practicing the goju-ryu kata - Sanchin.

The second factor to also affect the development of a style includes the personal beliefs, background and experiences of its founder. In order for a traditional style of *karate-do* to be accepted as legitimate, it must be globally accepted as having a unique perspective within the boundaries laid out by the *shorin* (Shuri-*te*) or *shorei* (Naha-*te*) schools. These two schools are considered to be the principal originators of traditional *karate-do* in Okinawa in the eighteenth century.

All *karate-do* styles espouse the doctrine of self-discipline, respect for life and proper ethical conduct. It takes the founder of a style a life-time of self-learning to

O-Sensei always states: 100% perspiration attains 10% inspiration!

fully embody these principles, and a strong moral conviction to be able to present these principles to others as a way of life that will help improve them physically, mentally and spiritually. Maintaining that one style of *karate-do* is better than another reduces a founder's lifetime of work to a purely technical venture and is a misguided and underdeveloped point of view.

The general public's view of hundreds of years of tradition can also be distorted by young sport-karate enthusiasts who believe they know all the answers after a few years of successful competition. These athletes go on to open chains of commercial schools that promote a "new style" of karate, but which generally consider tournament performance and monetary value to be the primary measures of success.

Each style of *karate-do* has specific methods and theories for presenting *kihon waza* conceptualized by the *shorin* and *shorei* schools. These provide the foundation, support and security for a *karate-ka* to rely on in a lifetime of training. *O-Sensei* has developed a means of presenting *kihon waza* principles so that *karate-ka* of all styles can understand the "hows" and "whys" of implementation. He has not developed any new *waza*, nor has he modified the mechanics or intent of any *kihon waza*. What he has been able to do is draw from any given technique the factors that determine the most efficient and effective methods of application. These methods uniquely benefit all human body structures and types. *O-Sensei* has spent decades developing these concepts so that young and old, frail and strong can progress without experiencing any needless sense of intimidation or protective hesitation. The elimination of these negative factors enables *karate-ka* to concentrate on working together to improve each other's *kihon waza* methodically and precisely. These techniques can then be effectively applied later on in *kumite* and *kata,* and also when a student is required to help instruct others.

O-Sensei corrects a student's posture.

Although every part of the human body can be trained as a defensive weapon, traditional *karate-do* bases a large part of training on the three main categories of *kihon waza*: blocking, striking and kicking. The strong execution of all of these depends in turn on strong *kihon-dachi* (basic stances). Within these categories and stances, *karate-ka* can explore *O-Sensei's* methods of application to best enhance technical proficiency. Each category below explores one of the key methods of application as a general overview of *O-Sensei's* training principles.

Uke Waza

As *karate-ka* rise through the ranks they learn different applications for the *uke waza* (blocking techniques) in their particular style. As beginners, they learn a certain block as a means of stopping an attack. This is usually practised as a hard, impacting technique focusing on powerful muscle contractions. With continued progress, students learn that *uke waza* can be employed as means of redirection, reducing the amount of power applied while at the same time maintaining control and composure. This becomes evident when practicing *kihon kumite* (basic sparring). Soon after, *karate-ka* are introduced to the use of *uke waza* for powerfully striking an attacker's limb as either a preemptive movement or a counter technique.

One of the keys to the focused application of all *uke waza* is the role the elbow plays in initiating a blocking sequence. After a full, strong set position has been adopted, the elbow must lead the rest of arm through the remainder of the technique. The important factor here is that a *karate-ka* must always fully

Helping a student lead with the elbow.

extend the elbow directly towards his/her opponent before the forearm is allowed to complete the blocking technique. The arms must stay as close as possible to the full-set position until the elbow has reached its maximum extension point.

Conceptually, this process seems simple enough to complete. It is actually more difficult in practice, however, as students have a tendency to concentrate on the end result. If an *uke waza* is rushed or forced with the sole intention of making

Finishing off the block with a snap of the wrist.

contact with the attacking arm, the shoulder will roll up and forward and the elbow will extend outward to the side of the body. This in turn causes the forearm to pull away from the center line of the body. The blocking arm should not reach out past the torso; it only needs to cover the area of the body under attack. When the elbow reaches out sideways past the torso, extra power is required to compensate for overextension and poor form. By extending the elbow forward instead, a student can complete an *uke waza* with a quick, sharp flick of the forearm or wrist, preventing imbalance and eliminating the need for excess force.

Having identified the elbow as the physical focus of all *uke waza*, a *karate-ka* can then explore the order of operation for completing a block. The physical motion of *uke waza* can be broken down into two stages. First is the retraction stage (setting). With inside-out blocks such as *uchi-uke* and *gedan-barai* (low block), the arms and torso must contract inwards without sacrificing posture and the shoulders should drop, allowing the body's center of gravity to settle lower. Once the retraction stage has been completed, the arms can be released to apply the block. The second stage, expansion (blocking), is where the elbows open up and the arms are allowed to expand to a completed block position.

With outside-in blocks such as *chudan soto-uke* (outside middle block) the process is reversed. In both cases, a low center of gravity must be maintained and the shoulders must remain relaxed and down to ensure good form and strong application. The order of operation for blocking works in conjunction with the tight-release principle outlined in Chapter 4.

Keri Waza

Keri waza (kicking techniques) seem to have the most diverse methods of application. This is not because there are a number of different ways of executing a kick, nor is it due to strategic concepts. The reason is that the complex anatomical makeup of the lower trunk and hip area makes each *karate-ka* vastly different. Factors such as flexibility, muscle density, bone length, body fat and age determine the ability to apply good, strong *keri waza*. More times than not, *karate-ka* subconsciously modify a kick's method of application due to physical limitations. It can prove quite a challenge to adhere to technical specifications laid down by past generations of *karate-do* instructors.

George Taylor and Leo Cossetto demonstrate a trapping (arm) and side kick combination.

Keri-waza must lead with the knee. This helps to force an opening in your opponents defense while improving your posture, timing and control.

The heel of the support leg must remain firmly on the ground for support and impacting focus.

Opposite page:
Top: David Tsuruoka demonstrates excellent speed and timing. As John Charry initiates a circular back kick, David drops to the floor and snaps a high round house kick to the groin with perfect "atemi".
Bottom: A technique found in the shotokan kata "Unsu".

Although all contributing factors - foot position, hip thrust, retraction, body angle, etc. - are vastly important for maintaining good form and control in *keri waza*, *O-Sensei* focuses on one area specifically to enhance kicking performance: the role the knee plays in executing a kick. This one area helps give all *karate-ka* a better chance to attain technical proficiency in such a demanding category.

The legs contribute a large amount of mass and weight to the overall make-up of the body. It is important for *karate-ka* to concentrate on good form and muscle control in order to move the weight of the legs quickly and efficiently to the intended target. *O-Sensei* points out that too many *karate-ka* focus on the end result of a kick. The kicking foot only makes contact with the target in the last portion of the technique - this is the area a *karate-ka* would least need to develop. The path a kick takes to the target is far more important to the technique itself and to

A good example of a high round house kick. Note the stability maintained by the supporting leg.

a student's overall development. The knee must therefore be looked at as a means of leading the kick to the point of impact. It must rise above the belt line before the foot is allowed to release, and the knee must thrust outward towards the target. The foot must fully retract after impact before the knee can be lowered below the waist to settle into a supporting stance.

This method of operation can be found in many styles of *karate-do*. The difference in Tsuruoka karate, however, is the focus on the knee *as the kick itself*. In other words, a *karate-ka* is expected to extend the leg as if the knee were actually going to hit the target. The foot is just an afterthought, used to transfer the power created by the knee to a point on the target.

The author practicing keri waza in a northern Canadian forest.

The emphasis on the knee has two beneficial effects. First, it allows the knee to be used for intimidation. As the knee thrusts towards an opponent, he/she will tend to react by shifting backwards. This opens up a cleared path for the kicking foot to impact with the target. Second, by emphasizing the thrust of the knee the student ensures that the kicking foot will swing forcefully out from under the thigh like a hammer. For optimum results using *mae-geri* (front kick), the foot should impact with a point one inch below the opponent's navel - this means the knee would have to thrust towards the opponent's upper abdominal area.

Wing Au, from the Newfoundland Tsuruoka dojo, initiates a dynamic front kick to his partner's mid-section.

A *karate-ka* developing *keri waza* by focusing on the role the knee plays develops excellent control through all phases of application. Supporting stances and balance also become stronger, increasing confidence in the areas of *kihon kumite* and *kata* as well.

Ate Waza

Ate waza (striking techniques) involve the hands and arms and offer a wide range of technical diversity. The elbows create crushing impact techniques, the wrist and palm areas offer rapid sweeping or circular techniques, the fists land like solid hammers and the fingers and knuckles pierce like spears or arrows. This wide range of techniques makes it difficult - but not impossible - to focus on only one of *O-Sensei's* key methods of application.

There is one application that unifies all striking techniques: the focused use of the *hikite* (pulling hand). As the use of the knee is singularly emphasized in all *keri waza*, so too is the pulling hand for all striking and blocking techniques. While a strong *hikite* is present in most styles of *karate-do*, *O-Sensei* believes this should actually be the main focus of attention for all striking techniques.

Even if a student tries to concentrate equally on what the striking arm and pulling hand are doing, the tendency is for attention to shift to impacting with the target or completing the technique. This shift in focus causes the weight of the body to shift forward, sacrificing composure and stability, and rendering impossible the application of the tight-release principle (see

Chapter 4). By concentrating on the pulling hand, a *karate-ka* retains balance and composure, remaining on center. At the same time, his/her technique becomes more fluid, allowing full application of the extension principle (also explained in Chapter 4).

By applying concentrated effort to the striking hand, a student risks throwing him/herself off balance. Too much applied effort in one direction without paying attention to all contributing factors can be detrimental in any situation. A simple example: many people suffer from back problems due to the stress placed on the lower back when attempting to lift heavy objects. Back problems can be avoided if an object is lifted with proper form and in the correct order of operation. It is true that heavy objects can often be lifted with the arms alone while bending at the waist, just as a punch can be thrown with the arm alone while rolling the shoulder forward. However, that same heavy object can be lifted much more easily and with less strain on the back if the person bends at the knees, keeps the back straight and lifts with the legs. Control is the main issue here: whether it is control of a heavy object or control over a strong punch, balance and stability must be maintained throughout.

O-Sensei helps a student correctly finish his punch.

Control is established by providing a reaction to every action. The heavy object directs weight downward and the legs provide the reaction of lifting upward. At a predetermined point the lifter presses upward to counteract the downward pressure of the object, concentrating solely on keeping balanced and stable. This should also hold true for a punch. As

When applied correctly, the "pulling hand" offers focus, stability, speed and composure.

the punching arm extends, the pulling arm should provide the reaction of retracting to the hips. If the punching and pulling hands finish with equal force and the stance is strong, a *karate-ka* should be able to remain balanced and stable, ready for the next action.

Another interesting point is: which areas require attention as the object is lifted or the punch is thrown? In the former case, one factor remains constant: the object will always exert pressure downwards. This means the lifter need not be concerned with this part of the equation. Instead, he/she can concentrate completely on the act of lifting up with the legs, trusting that the downward pressure will always be there. This also holds true for all *ate waza*. The constant factor here is the fact that a punch or strike is heading for a target - this is a subconscious reaction to danger which does not usually require conscious control. Therefore, if a technique has been previously practised and performed well enough, a *karate-ka* can put the striking hand out of his/her mind and concentrate on the pulling hand, which helps make a *karate-do tsuki* so effective.

Kihon-Dachi

Kihon-dachi (basic stances) play a critical role in a *karate-ka*'s overall performance. The relationship between stance and technique should be discussed first so that physical considerations can be extended to questions of attitude, spirit and strategy.

In Tsuruoka karate - as in all traditional styles - stances are considered to be the basis for binding all physical elements together. This is reflected in the relationship between motion and stability. The stability factor in all *karate-do* movements is the earth, ground or supporting structure - this forms the platform for all techniques and strategies, and should be considered as much a part of the *karate-ka* as the legs are. Motion cannot occur without the earth providing something to push away from or contract towards. *Kihon-dachi* are designed to develop the strongest possible connection between the earth and technique.

Tsuruoka *karate-ka* study three main factors within each stance. Compression is the first factor. This involves a feeling of built-up tension or energy within the stance which must be released in one quick burst. The muscles should have a feeling of tight retraction, just on the verge of exploding in the direction

Makiwara training at the Hombu Dojo: an excellent means for correcting form, posture and focus. The makiwara helps a student "feel" the conection between the technique, the stance and the earth.

of intent. Compression should be felt most strongly in one's personal *kumite-dachi* (sparring stance). This allows a *karate-ka* to move as quickly as possible, without any excess jerky body movement which would reveal intent to an opponent.

Pressure is the second factor. This is used to transfer the stability of the earth to a *karate-do* posture. Pressure for each stance is applied at different locations of the body and allows a student to hold firmly to his/her position. Defensively, pressure and stability prevent a *karate-ka* from being overwhelmed or forced off balance. Offensively, pressure aids in controlling techniques and inhibiting over-commitment, especially when counterattacking.

The third factor, contraction, is the only one concerned with motion from one stance to the next. When a student pushes forward or back to change position without using contraction, he/she is using only one leg to do so. This means muscle power in the other leg is used only for stabilizing support after the step has been completed. This is not an efficient use of muscle power.

Utilizing contraction, on the other hand, requires both legs to draw together. Direction in a step forward or back is determined by which leg is left on the ground. If the front leg remains the step is forward, if the back leg remains the step is backwards. Utilizing the power of both legs means less energy is wasted, movement is faster and more refined and posture remains composed.

Contraction also helps eliminate tell-tale signs that telegraph the imminent launching of a technique. One of the most difficult motions to prevent is the action of the front foot flipping outward just before a step forward is taken, seen mostly when moving in *zenkutsu-dachi* (front stance). Contraction stops this outward foot rotation by containing the push-off motion until the last quarter of the step.

The heel of the foot plays an important part in these processes as it ties stances and techniques to the earth. All the compression, extension and contraction in the world will not

Zenkutsu-dachi (front stance)

Right: *Maintaining posture is paramount for creating stability. The front knee must be over the foot but must not extend past the middle of the arch.*

Bottom left: *Note the front knee position. The heel of the foot, the knee and the hip all line up. This is the correct form for maintaining a stable and balanced front stance.*

Bottom right: *In this photo the knee is pushed too far outward. The leg creates a bowing effect releasing support, and the foot rolls onto it's outside edge reducing contact area with the floor. This is a common mistake that can be corrected over time.*

work if the heel is allowed to lift from the ground. The heel allows the legs to function as supporting braces for a stance, which in turn increases the effects of *kime*.

Contraction will also not work if the heel is allowed to flip upwards as a step is initiated - a raised heel means a weak leg that cannot be used to contract. This would also risk throwing a technique out of its proper order of operation or execution. It should be noted that raising the heels slightly due to compression and lifting or flipping the heels due to poor form are two different things. A slightly raised heel due to compression is acceptable - especially during *kumite* - provided the ankle has already been flexed to the maximum.

All three factors work together with O-Sensei's *kihon* principles (see Chapter 4) in the order of operation presented above. Once a stance has been assumed, outward pressure should be applied to the legs. The feeling at this point should be as though one is straddling a deep ravine: if outward pressure were released, one would fall down into the ravine. When pressure is strong, compression comes into play. Compression builds up the energy to explode in a given direction and throw oneself clear of the ravine.

Compression must remain constant throughout the stance, but contraction should replace pressure once one has gathered the confidence to leap clear of the ravine. Outward pressure on the edges of the supporting earth must be released and the legs immediately contracted to pull oneself to safety (the leg in the direction of intended movement remains firmly on the ledge).

One must be careful at this point not to push too hard off the other ledge with the trailing leg; this would cause the earth to crumble underfoot and precipitate a fall. With the heels kept firmly down to hold the earth in place, early compression and the subsequent pull of contraction can be trusted to shift oneself to a safe location.

Kokutsu-dachi (back stance)

Top: This is the correct posture for back stance. The heel, knee and hips of the back leg all line up to form a strong support brace. The tanden (lower abdomen) drops to lower the center of gravity, and the shoulders line up with the hips.

Bottom: This is a poor representation of back stance. The back leg bows outward releasing support, the hips and tanden (lower abdomen) sit up too high, the feet are too wide apart and the shoulders lean too far back.

Kiba-dachi *(straddle stance)*

Top left: *Contraction of the inner thigh muscles and the lower tanden create a strong stance from all directions. The center of the patella (knee cap) should line up vertically with the inside edge of the foot.*

Top Right: *This posture is incorrect. The legs are too wide apart, and bow excessively.*

Bottom left: *Demonstrating the correct angle of the hips after the tanden is allowed to drop.*

Bottom right: *The hips are tucked too far under the torso, raising the center of gravity.*

Kihon-Dachi and *Zanshin*

O-Sensei often stresses the development of strong *zanshin*, so much so that his students frequently practise a form of strategic *kumite* that does not include the use of any *kihon waza*. Instead, *karate-ka* must rely on *zanshin*, eye contact and intimidating stances to control their partners. An intimidating stance is not any kind of secret new technique but is a method of overall strategic presentation. Two *karate-ka* face off with the goal of forcing each other to flinch, shift or react to something other than a physical technique. As partners stare at and analyze each other, they look for means of breaking their partner's concentration. This break in concentration (*suki*) is usually enough to cause one partner to shift or flinch, giving the other partner the opportunity to attack.

O-Sensei's projection of zanshin always proves intimidating.

An Authoritative posture, focused intent and concentration of facial features can all be used to throw off an opponent. However, using pressure, compression and contraction as explained above can also prove extremely useful in distracting an opponent. Compression is used especially often to project *zanshin* or intent to cause an opponent to waver. In the exercise above, shifting and stepping back and forth at any speed is allowed as long as the stepping motion itself is not used as intimidation. In other words, stepping or shifting must be used as a nonthreatening rhythmic motion only, allowing presentation of the stance itself to provoke reaction.

Kumite Dachi

A simple definition of *kumite-dachi* would combine the basic stances learned in the first few years of training into one generic stance. However, there is no set standard as to which percentage each stance should account for in an individual's fighting posture - this makes a *kumite-dachi* a very personal thing for each *karate-ka*. A number of factors could determine a sparring stance. For example, someone with strong *yoko-geri* could incorporate a higher percentage of *kiba-dachi* (horse stance) in his/her *kumite-dachi*; a defensive fighter might employ more *kokutsu-dachi* (back stance).

Although sparring stances develop differently based on individual strengths and weaknesses, *O-Sensei* believes it is important for *karate-ka* to begin with one generic *kumite- dachi*. From here individuals will, in time, gradually develop their own stance. *O-Sensei* stresses that a *kumite-dachi* should be one that can be adopted almost instantaneously, explaining that on the street there is often little time or room to drop into a solid low stance, or even to shift or adjust weight. A sparring stance should thus be as easy to adopt as walking down the street.

O-Sensei demonstrates this principle in the *dojo* by walking a few steps and then sinking down with one foot approximately eight inches in front of the other. He illustrates the pressure, compression, contraction and hip thrust (see below) which can be drawn from this compact but dynamic stance by walking up to a bigger student deeply rooted in *zenkutsu-dachi*. He places a hand on the student's chest - the student is sent toppling backwards but *O-Sensei* appears only to have sunk down a few inches.

Tsuruoka Hip Thrust

Hip thrust is used in conjunction with a stance's compression factor. It was developed by *O-Sensei* as a means of forcing a *kumite-dachi* into its maximum compression point. Hip thrust speeds up the transition from a static position to stance contraction and subsequent directional stepping or shifting. It is also used as an intimidation factor and as a means of closing distance.

Hip thrust works for both an attacker and a defender. An attacker prepares his/her stance to launch a technique. Once compression has been achieved, the side of the pelvic bone over the front leg thrusts forward and rotates slightly upward. This causes the glutius muscles above the rear leg to contract and the torso to fully line up with the center of the pelvic bone. At this point, the weight of the body is centralized, allowing limbs to be quickly and freely thrown in any attack. Hip thrust

Left: *A sparring stance without hip thrust.*

Right: *A sparring stance with hip thrust applied.*

also places the pelvic bone closer to an opponent to help close the distance when attacking.

For a defender, shifting the pelvic bone forward allows the rear leg to contract quickly by favorably redistributing weight. The rear leg pulls back easily from under the torso, allowing the rest of the body to retract quickly and smoothly. For beginners, *O-Sensei* includes hip thrust in a separate order of operations, counting out each part individually, for example, "Step! Pressure! Compress! Thrust! Contract-Release!"

Hip Rotation

Hip rotation is the action of rotating the hip horizontally from an "open" to a "closed" position or vice versa. Rotation from "closed" to "open" is used for techniques such as blocking, jabbing and kicking. Rotation from "open" to "closed" occurs in such techniques as lunge punches, reverse punches and front kicks from the back leg. Hip rotation is extremely important for proper technical application: it not only aids in strong *kime* but also lengthens an applied technique, strengthens good posture and generates a greater range of directional movement.

Left: *Hips in the open position.*   Right: *Hips in the closed position.*

Hip Vibration

Hip vibration is an important part of completing such techniques as *uke waza* and *ate waza*. Its purpose is to aid the projection of *kime* by completely contracting the muscles in the hip area. This results in solid unification between the upper and lower body. Vibration is performed by sharply pivoting the hips from one horizontal direction to the other within a range no greater than two inches. This, however, should only be performed as a slight shudder which feels completely natural. Over-emphasis of hip vibration can prove very detrimental to the outcome of a technique.

Beginners are introduced to the mechanics of hip vibration through the hip-lock principle outlined in the next chapter. The hip-lock principle should be continually applied - as any *kihon waza* should - to ensure that hip vibration generates the maximum focusing effects.

Tsuruoka Sensei always stresses the importance of the hips!

Tsuruoka Kihon Principles

4

The Hip-Lock Principle

The hip-lock principle developed by *O-Sensei* is a relatively new concept based on an old principle. It is a method of instructing beginners which in turn affords greater appreciation and understanding by the intermediate student as he/she progresses.

Since the early days in Okinawa, one of the most important factors in *karate-do* training has been the role the hip area plays in improving speed, strength, focus, balance and stability. Learning correct applications for hip vibration and hip rotation can be a long and arduous task, one which needs to be personally experienced from within each *karate-ka* to be fully understood.

The perceived problem here is that karate was developed by Asian people for Asian physiques and psyches. It is difficult for other people to learn and teach an art created in a culture

Practicing hip lock with a partner.

very different from their own, especially if there are considerable physical differences involved. In proportionate terms, Westerners are generally taller and longer in bone with a higher center of gravity.[1] In addition, Western society generally considers people to be stronger and physically superior when they have large upper-body mass and breathe high into the chest cavity. This cultural focus on the upper body as the source of physical power is an obstacle which many Western *karate-ka* find difficult to overcome at first.

Nevertheless, there are several examples of lower-body emphasis within Western culture as well. Athletes such as power lifters, Olympic wrestlers, soccer and rugby players, etc. consider the notion of the upper body as the main source of power to be misguided. Closer to home, almost everyone would recognize the negative effects of lifting a heavy object with the arms (upper body) instead of with the legs (lower body). Whatever their background or experience, *karate-ka* must recognize the importance of the lower body as this is what affords free movement, provides balance and support and generates initial power through contact with the ground.

O-Sensei demonstrates power from the hips at summer camp in Coboconk, Ontario.

The place where lower-body strength and mobility connect to upper-body movement and extension of force is the largest bone in the body - the hip-bone. If one learns to engage the hip properly - contracting the muscles around it to the maximum and instantly releasing when necessary - one will be able to control movement of the entire body like a finely-tuned machine or a top-of-the-line computer.

The hip-lock principle breaks down the role the hips play during the practice of *karate-do*. It is introduced to junior *karate-ka* (approximately fourth *kyu*) when working on *kihon* or *kata*, but should be fully extended to all areas of advanced training as well. It will take quite some time before the benefits can be seen in all areas of performance, but once the principle has been internalized, the improvements in control, speed, timing and stability are undeniable.

All basic punches and strikes employ the hip-lock principle by rotating the pelvic bone horizontally in the opposite direction of the arm executing the technique, one to two seconds after the arm has focused the strike. This rotation must be sharp, crisp and strong - using peak muscle contraction in the hip area only - and must be held until the next strike. The pause or time delay between the strike and hip lock is critical. This is the moment when the overall tension in the body must relax or settle in order to lower one's center of gravity and shoulders. The feeling should be as though all body weight is relocating to the hip area. When the next strike is initiated, the compression generated by the hip lock is released to allow for a quick explosive movement - much like a sprinter who is tensed up and waiting to release upon hearing the starter pistol - and then the process begins again. The process is the same

Contemplating results.

for all blocks and extended strikes (such as the jab), except that the hip rotates and thrusts out in the same direction as the arm executing the technique.

Over time, the hip-lock action occurs simultaneously with the applied technique. *Karate-ka* can regularly refer to and practice this training breakdown to keep all *kihon waza* strong and focused.

The Tight-Release Principle

The tight-release principle is used to enhance technical execution. Practitioners of any Asian combative sport or art are always searching for ways to perform techniques without giving away intent or timing. They strive to enter in past a partner's defenses by reducing his/her opportunity to react. Towards this end, *karate-ka* are instructed to initiate techniques from the hip (see hip-lock principle above).

As mentioned previously, it is not always easy for Westerners to grasp this concept as their society tends to focus on the upper body. For example, carpentry saws and military swords "push" from the upper torso to cut. In Japanese society, however, these implements cut on a "pull" stroke. Pulling actions rely more on the lower body and hips, whereas pushing actions depend heavily on the shoulders to complete a given task. The difficulty for Western *karate-ka* is to abandon ingrained "push" strategies and allow themselves to learn new approaches.

People with large upper-body mass have the hardest time trying to lead a technique with

Just before the point of release.

the hips and not with the shoulders. When the shoulders are relied on for power and motion, three problems occur:

(1) Intent is revealed, allowing an opponent time to escape and set up a counter technique. The shoulders are so close to an opponent's line of vision that they are often the first things he/she sees.

(2) The large amount of weight in the shoulder area can easily throw off a person's balance. Even the slightest displacement of weight leads to overcommitment, preventing the application of the hip-lock principle to stabilize the stance and overall composure. Over-commitment of technique can be very dangerous when facing someone adept at takedowns or grappling techniques.

(3) Technique is disrupted by throwing off the order of execution.

A reverse punch follows this basic order of execution:
- back leg presses from the ground
- hip rotates from pressure created in the stance
- striking arm rotates with the hip (pulling hand retracts)
- punch is extended with the force generated by the hips.

This traditional method of execution keeps the punch on the correct path to the target, with the elbows in and down, knuckles in line with forearm and hip rotation preceding arm extension. As soon as the shoulders are allowed to move first, however, the arm extends before the hip, the elbow flips out, the heel lifts off the floor (leaning the body forward) and the punch becomes more of a circular technique as opposed to a linear one.

The tight-release principle is introduced at the intermediate level (around second *kyu*) to help eliminate shoulder extension during a punch, such as described above. The concept calls for tight compression when pulling back to set, and for quick release from the hip when extending to strike - these actions are similar to those employed when drawing a bow and releasing an arrow. In both cases, strength and compression are present

Top and Bottom: *O-Sensei demonstrates the penetrating effects of the tight-release principle.*

in the pull phase only. When the arrow or technique is released, there is no longer any strength, pressure or dynamics applied - the weapon simply extends to pierce its target.

The *karate-do* punch is thus meant to penetrate - not club - an object. The energy generated should appear to extend beyond the physical limit of the arm and on through the back of the target. This power flow is further analyzed in association with the extension principle discussed next.

The Extension Principle

While teaching class, *O-Sensei* rarely refers to a linear closed-fist strike as simply the act of punching. He constantly guides students toward the meaning of the technique by having them extend the arm rather than overcommit to the application. Instead of saying "Set! Block! Punch!" to count off a combination technique, he will often call, "Set! Block! Extend!"

O-Sensei notes that when the majority of people execute a technique their *kime* or intent is directed at the surface of the target. As a student tries to increase impact with the surface, the punching shoulder rotates and the lead elbow flips outward. A *karate-do* strike is actually meant to extend *kime* behind the surface of the target - students should remember not to rely on arm length alone to determine the point of focus or impact.

This basic concept is taught as early as sixth *kyu* as a good introduction to extension. However, the principle involves more than just focusing an attack somewhere behind a target - it is more a centered state of mind that guides physical intent. Unfortunately much gets lost in

O-Sensei tests a stance after the extension principle has be applied.

the interpretation as *karate-ka* develop over the years.

One reason for this may be incomplete awareness while practicing *kihon waza*. Performing basics *"in air"* removes the distraction of a solid target surface and allows students to stretch techniques to their physical limits. However, as *O-Sensei* sees it, extension has nothing to do with physical limits but is determined instead by what happens after a technique has been carried out.

Once a thrust has been completed and proper *kime* has been applied, mental concentration is extended past the point where physical contact would be made and out further along the direction of intent. This keeps *kime* strong and is closely linked to good *zanshin*. By continuing with mental extension, *kime* and *zanshin*, a *karate-ka* makes the strike as dynamic as possible while at the same time inhibiting any strong counter-attack by the opponent.

Karate-ka must eventually be able to apply a technique to an actual physical target as if there were no striking surface in front of them. When they are ready, students will want to practice maintaining this frame of mind while hitting the *makiwara* (striking post). A word of caution: this will not be effective if the technique is weak in any way, and personal injury may occur if *kihon waza* and/or *zanshin* are poor. *Karate-ka* must therefore be diligent in perfecting their technique and refining their concentration.

Of course, extension alone does not make an effective technique. Also important is the contribution of the body, which should radiate composure and add solidification in the direction of intent. The added support of the body increases the stability and focus of the technique while decreasing "bounce-back" vibration (recoil). The combined effects of a well-anchored body and focused extension ensure greater target penetration and increased potential for internal damage.

The extension principle is initially presented using thrusting techniques but is also applied to snapping techniques once the basic concept has been grasped. Application of the principle

Top and bottom: *The author demonstrates basic aikido techniques.*

remains much the same for snapping techniques, except that the striking part will be retracted from the target instead of remaining extended. Mental extension, *kime* and *zanshin* should continue to be projected well after the striking part has been snapped back.

The concept of mental extension in the direction of intent can also be seen in the Japanese martial art of *aikido*, a discipline which relies on harmony with the surroundings. An *aikido-ka* (practitioner) uses a partner's own energy against him/herself to perform a circular throw or takedown to gain control of a threatening technique. *Aikido-ka* practice lowering their center of gravity and focusing extension downward through the ground. The founder of *aikido*, Morihei Ueshiba *Sensei*, was superb at

controlling his partners through his ability to relax and extend a mental connection to the ground - many students would collectively try to throw their teacher off balance but to no avail. Old film footage shows the master's ability to extend *ki* (energy) for stability and technical application.

One of Ueshiba *Sensei*'s top students, Koichi Tohei *Sensei*, went on to develop a system for practicing *ki* principles based on his teacher's original findings. This commitment to mental extension and concentration on Tohei *Sensei*'s part illustrates the importance of further exploring the role that extension and the mind play in *budo* training methods.

Kihon Waza Overview

Kihon waza provide the foundation for all concepts which follow in any martial art. Learning to walk before one can run is an accurate model to begin with. Walking and *kihon waza* are both learned by repeating movements over and over again. Learners in both cases subconsciously discover through repetition the most efficient method of execution, which in turn minimizes fatigue, stress and discomfort.

Once running has been mastered, walking is neither forgotten or abandoned. In fact, the more someone runs the more he/she counts on walking to complete the journey. For example, someone who has suffered a back or leg injury relies on the therapeutic coordination processes of basic walking to heal his/herself. An injured *karate-ka* may similarly ease him/herself back into training by performing *kihon waza* slowly and loosely at first.

The initial motivation for learning basic physical techniques - walking, eating, writing, blocking, punching, etc. - is generally to achieve a tangible goal or destination. For example, walking gets one somewhere, eating nourishes the body, writing communicates information, blocking and punching defend against pain. There is another side to these basics, however, which professionals and hobbyists study to enrich their understanding and appreciation of a larger perspective.

Just as walking, eating and writing can be used to share experiences and enjoy the fellowship of others, *kihon waza* can be used by intermediate and advanced *karate-ka* to explore balance, timing and cooperation with others.

Karate-do techniques were developed so that anyone could learn and apply them after a reasonable period of study. The applications of *kihon waza* are frequently practiced in *kata* and are apparently powerful enough to be effective in most confrontations. In *jiyu-kumite* (free sparring), the most likely techniques to score are also the most basic: *gyaku-zuki, mae-geri* and *kizami-zuki*. Strong fundamentals thus play an important role in all aspects of *karate-do* practice and applications.

In order to develop good *kihon waza*, the individual must be willing to change to fit the art. Unfortunately, human nature tends to seek the simplest solution to any given challenge. Too often this means cutting corners and reducing practice time, while hoping to achieve the same results, i.e., changing the art to suit the individual. This is where problems begin to surface.

Diligent practice and testing. The life of a karate-ka.

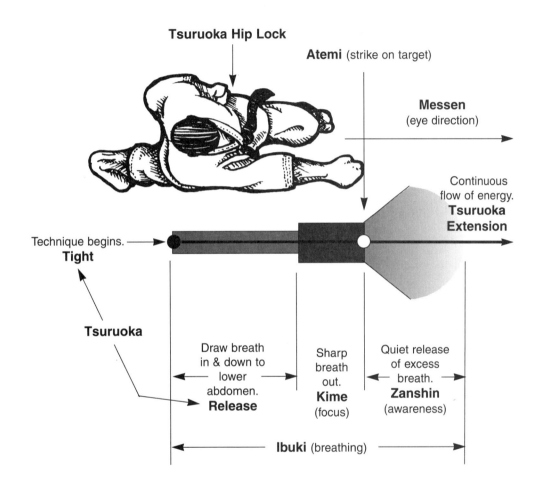

Application of "Karate-do Constant Principles" & "Tsuruoka Kihon Principles".

A student who is too impatient to learn the correct technique may happen upon an easier method which complements their physique and seems to achieve the desired results. This individual then goes off to try and teach this "new technique" to others, not realizing that other body types will not necessarily respond in the same way to the new method. Such offshoots of "rushed self-discovery" are frequently the basis of overtly commercialized "martial arts."

While traditional *karate-do* stresses the importance of building up solid *kihon waza*, it does eventually allow freedom of expression in the more advanced applications of these techniques. Methods of sparring - from *gohon* to *sanbon* to *jiyu-kumite* - allow a *karate-ka* to explore strategy and timing and develop his/her own personal variations (see Chapter 6).

O-Sensei enjoys teaching children, helping them develop discipline, coordination and confidence.

O-Sensei demonstrates the importance of basics with the help of Mas Takano.

Nevertheless, the foundation for reaching this self-exploration stage has always been strong *kihon waza*. It is thus very important that a *karate-ka* hold true to the basic techniques and values instilled by his/her *sensei*. Traditional movements and form should remain as they were originally conceived: many years were put into their development for the purposes of generating good health and effective execution. Each *karate-ka* should strive to ensure that these techniques will be available in their pure form for generations to come.

Kata and Kumite

型と組み手

5

Kata and *kumite* were developed to apply *kihon waza* to interaction between two or more people. Both must be equally recognized and practiced by all traditional *karate-ka* for a fuller understanding of the art and the perpetuation of personal growth. *Kata* and *kumite* must therefore remain connected through their theoretical, technical and spiritual aspects.

Kata: Purpose and Practice

After some *kihon waza* have been introduced to a beginner, their applications are linked and practiced in *kata*. Present in each style of *karate-do*, *kata* offer the student imaginary scenarios in which to employ a variety of techniques. *Karate-ka* thus learn how to move, step and react in response to a number of different possible attacks. *Kata* offer safe means of learning how to defend oneself, while at the same time giving each student the chance to use and develop his/her imagination.

The original *bunkai* (breakdown and interpretation of *kata* combinations) which accompany all *kata* techniques provide an overall starting point, then continue to challenge the student by offering further opportunities for new *bunkai* to be developed at the personal level. New *bunkai* must never displace the original, but should be constantly encouraged to keep *kata* relevant to all those who wish to continue learning and exploring.

Kata are presented in two main themes of study. One of these explores power, strength and stability. *Kata* in this group are used to develop composure and strong defensive postures,

David Tsuruoka instructing advanced kata

and to increase muscle and bone mass. The second theme explores speed, balance and sharp directional movement. *Kata* in this group sharpen reflexes and timing, and develop rhythm.

All junior-level *kata* within a *karate-do* system contain movements beneficial to all body types (see Chapter 3). As *karate-ka* advance, they will notice the *kata* developing many more specific themes or scenarios that would benefit one body type more than another. For example, the *shotokan kata-Empi* (swooping swallow) utilizes very quick techniques and numerous stance changes that move a *karate-ka* through many varying directions, not just forward and back, left and right. This *kata* would best suit a person of smaller stature, allowing him/her to practice

Left: *Glen Kawaguchi of British Columbia demonstrates the 1st move of the shotokan kata-Empi.*
Right: *Ron Fagan of Nova Scotia demonstrates the 1st move of the shotokan kata-Heian nidan.*

sharp defensive reactions against powerful attacks. The *shotokan kata Tekki shodan* (iron rider) features powerful thrusting techniques designed to benefit a heavier-set, less mobile individual.

History of *Kata*

Many martial arts around the world incorporate *kata* into their training methods, though with varying degrees of emphasis. Some systems, such as Korean tae-kwon-do, Chinese *ch'uan-fa* or kung fu and Japanese *kendo* (fencing), explore *kata* in similar fashion to *karate-do*. Other systems such as Chinese *t'ai chi ch'uan* and Japanese *iaido* (sword-drawing), use *kata* as their sole means of training.

However, *karate-do*'s particular relationship to *kata* goes well beyond physical training applications. The intense love for *kata* and the desire to perform them distinguish *karate-ka*

Contemplating the shotokan kata - Sochin.

from most other martial artists. To them, a *kata* is more than a series of prearranged moves designed to improve technique. It is a vessel for the human spirit's instinct and determination for survival.

When Okinawans were forbidden to carry weapons in earlier times, karate would have been considered a threat to Japanese security. The art thus had to be practiced in complete secrecy. Students would often retreat to the mountains at night and train in caves or in dense forests. The Okinawans' determination for "survival through secrecy" deterred anyone from keeping precise written records of karate's development. *Kata* thus became the means for passing the art from teacher to student, from generation to generation. Without *kata*, large amounts of *karate-do*'s history and character would have been lost forever.

A few other martial arts also have a suppressed history. *Capoeira*, a Brazilian martial art which uses acrobatic skills to confuse and defeat an opponent, was banned by the colonial government in the sixteenth century. It was subsequently "hidden" in a religious dance by slaves who needed some kind of defense against the brutal slave traders of that period. *Capoeira* is still practiced today within a ceremonial dance: students flip, cartwheel and kick to the sounds and tempo of the *berimbau* (a bow-shaped instrument). Filipino martial arts also had to be practiced in complete secrecy during the seventeenth and eighteenth centuries when strict Spanish rule banned weapons or any form of military training.

Tsuruoka Practical-Application *Kata*

Reflecting Okinawa's historical challenge, many karate techniques and *kata* were developed to defend against weapons. Several were applied by stepping into an attacker to smother any chance of using a weapon (see *sen-no-sen* in Chapter 7). Today, attacks by *katana* (swords) or *naginata* (halberds) are rare, so new *bunkai* have been developed to fit the existing *kata*.

O-Sensei has taken this one step further and developed exercises that modify existing *kata* to fit possible applications in the modern world. Modifications are not found in the technical movements themselves, but rather in the direction of each step taken or stance adopted. These adaptations are deliberately referred to here as *exercises*. In no way does O-Sensei wish to change the history of karate *kata*: original forms must continue to be practiced, perfected and handed down to the next generation. *O-Sensei's* purpose here is actually to reinforce understanding and appreciation of existing *kata* by introducing an additional dimension to their performance. Many traditional instructors have their students practice *kata* from the last move to the first, from right to left, with hands reversed, etc. - this helps students remember movements and prevents them from favoring one side over another.

O-Sensei's practical-application exercises give *karate-ka* a chance to practice *bunkai* at different *maai* (distances from their opponents). For example, the first two movements in *Heian-shodan* have traditionally been to step to the left into *zenkutsu-dachi* (front stance) with *gedan-barai* (low block), then step again in the same direction with *oi-zuki* (lunge punch). For the same two movements, *O-Sensei* asks students to first step back to the right (facing left) with *gedan-barai* - blocking an attack from a safe distance - and then continuing in to strike the attacker with *oi-zuki*. The *kata* continues with the same format of first stepping away from the attack then following through with the counter. All *kata* can be practiced in this manner, improving technique and broadening comprehension.

Opposite page:
Top: *A basic shotokan kata using the traditional method of stepping forward, into the attack.*

Bottom: *The same kata is demonstrated using O-Sensei's practical application exercise of stepping away from an attack.*

Kata and Personal Growth

Karate-ka must continuously strive to master the *kata* of their particular style. This involves perfecting not only form and posture, but also composure, timing, *bunkai* and character.

Perfection of form: *kata* are the perfect means to learn and apply the key principles of *kihon waza* (see Chapter 2). *Ibuki* can be practiced through the transition from one movement to the next. *Atemi* can be developed with proper posture and in the correct order of execution. *Messen* can improve balance, aid strategic intent and enhance the presentation of the *kata*. Utilizing the power of the hips through rotation, vibration, thrusting and locking will help cement the relationship between form and composure.

Tom Pryde of Burlington, Ontario, demonstrating the shotokan kata - Sochin.

Perfection of composure: This one of the most difficult goals for a Tsuruoka *karate-ka* to attain. Students work on using *O-Sensei's* three principles of tight-release, extension and hip-lock to strengthen stability and focus. These can be developed with the help of a partner: if correct form and composure work in unison, a *karate-ka* should be able to hold a stance and extend a technique while a partner tests him/her by pushing and pressing on certain points of his/her body. These points differ from stance to stance and are tested to help to develop the correct pressure and compression for each stance. A *karate-ka* should be able to resist strong pressure and maintain a low center of gravity while keeping his/her facial and shoulder muscles completely relaxed.

Perfection of timing: Correct timing helps a student develop a relationship between composure and the transition from one technique to the next. Far too many *karate-ka* misinterpret the need for fast, sharp movements to mean rushing through a *kata's* performance. The pace and timing of a *kata* can be relatively calm or slow, punctuated with quick, sharp techniques. Students must remember that a *kata* is meant to tell a story. If someone reading a story out loud were to rush through the words in a monotone voice, the listener would soon lose interest and understanding. A storyteller must embellish words, fill the narrative with feeling and vary tones of voice in order to capture and hold the interest of an audience. The same holds true for *kata* performance, even if there are not always spectators present. A *karate-ka* should be able to feel the emotion, spirit and fluctuating intensity of a *kata* him/herself in order to completely understand its timing, energy and meaning.

Martin Hung applies the 1st movement from the shotokan kata - Heian nidan to defend against a lunge punch.

Perfection of bunkai: Bunkai, along with timing, give a *kata* its true meaning. *Karate-ka* must know the breakdown or significance of each series of movements in a *kata*. Once a basic *bunkai* has been established, a student should be able to apply it with either hand or foot to either side. It should also be practiced to the point where it can be performed spontaneously. This offers a transition from *kata* to *kumite*, showing the relationship among all types of *karate-do* training. *Kihon waza* take formerly alien concepts and turn them into reflex actions. *Kata* sharpen responses into spontaneous reflexes. *Kumite* then takes these spontaneous reactions and produces strategic planning.

Perfection of character: Constant *kata* practice yields a strong spirit through perseverance, a clear mind through

Kyu belts, led by Andy Horbatuik, practice the shotokan kata-Heian sandan

concentration and an open heart through helping one's classmates. These attributes should permeate all aspects of a *karate-ka*'s life. Gichin Funakoshi, the founder of modern *karate-do*, repeatedly stated that "the spirit of *karate-do* is lost without courtesy."[1] At the beginning and end of every *kata*, performers bow to show respect to teachers, observers, imaginary opponents, and the spirit of *karate-do* itself. Through the setting of goals, the overcoming of personal hardship and the support of one's peers, students learn to fully respect themselves and others. Lack of this respect could later result in tremendous damage being inflicted in *kumite*; as *karate-ka* begin to realize this they move from an initial appreciation of karate as a form of self-defense to a personal understanding of the importance of self-awareness and moral development.

Kata can only be perfected through constant repetition. Only after fully immersing him/herself in a *kata* can a student begin to discover the vast knowledge hidden in its movements. *Karate-ka* thus learn to respect and embrace the patience and dedication required by their art.

Top and Bottom: *Black belts performing the shotokan kata-Nijushiho in small groups at the Tsuruoka Canadian Budokai Hombu Dojo in Toronto.*

Kumite: Purpose and Practice

Karate-do is a cumulative program of study. Although *karate-ka* go through many stages of development - from beginner to advanced student and possibly on to instructor - anything learned will never become obsolete or inconsequential. *Kihon waza* and *kata* can be looked at as building blocks which form a carefully constructed foundation for *kumite* to follow. These building blocks can neither be removed nor allowed to deteriorate, or the entire "structure" will collapse, i.e., *kumite* will suffer.

A relatively new method of training in modern *karate-do*, *jiyu-kumite* can be considered a long-term strategic goal for beginners. It must never exceed *kihon* and *kata* in importance but should instead receive an equal level of emphasis throughout a *karate-ka*'s career. Incorporating strong *kata* techniques into *kumite* is an excellent method of simulating the timing, reflexes and reactions that might occur in an actual confrontation where a student's skills would be relied on to avoid injury and/or preserve life.

Tom Pryde performs a leg sweep during jiyu-kumite.

Jiyu-kumite was devised and first introduced to the general Japanese populace in 1936 by the head of *goju-ryu karate-do*, Gogen Yamaguchi.[2] This is a relatively late start when compared to judo and *kendo*, possibly reflecting the fact that early *karate-ka* had always practiced their art in the spirit in which it was initially intended, i.e., for self-preservation, possibly to the point of maiming or killing an adversary. Some modifications were obviously necessary before karate could be presented at goodwill sporting events.

Practitioners in a few karate systems - such as the Japanese *koei-kan* - utilize *bogu* (armor) similar to that worn by *kendo-ka* (fencers) when engaging in *kumite*. This allows the application of truly penetrating techniques with little risk of injury. In American karate or kickboxing, protagonists wear padded hand and foot gear. They compete in a system very similar to Western boxing with full-contact circular punches and kicks, although no knee or elbow techniques are permitted. Most traditional *karate-ka*, however, engage in noncontact *kumite*.

Reactions and physical confidence improve as partners move around each other while sparring, shifting and stepping for strategic advantage. Self-defense techniques can be simulated in various scenarios with different conclusions. As physical improvement takes place, *karate-ka* begin to develop stronger perseverance and determination. *Kumite* thus offers many ways for *karate-ka* to grow physically, strategically and psychologically.

There is one very large hurdle at this point that all modern *karate-ka* must overcome before they can be said to have discovered the spirit of *budo* (the way of the warrior): the shortcomings of the human ego. Sadly, as societies change and as the art of karate evolves further, the ego factor seems to be the one key concept most often avoided by students and instructors alike, especially in a commercial *dojo*. The two most likely reasons for this are (1) these aspects are very difficult to explore, understand and control, (2) they are easily neglected in today's economic society where the emphasis is so heavily placed on pure physical fitness as a means to alleviate stress.

Practicing jiyu-ippon kumite

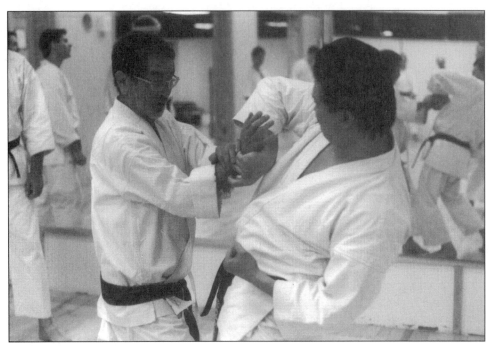
O-Sensei demonstrates an effective wrist lock.

It should be noted that ego involves both positive and negative attributes, as duality expressed in the Chinese concept of *yin* and *yang*. Positive attributes produce confidence and stature, helping a *karate-ka* to develop into a sound technician and, eventually, a good teacher. Negative attributes allow anger to dominate, clouding judgment and weakening strategy. If the negative aspects of the ego are not controlled during *kumite*, strength replaces tactics, "brawling" takes over and people get seriously hurt.

Novices begin their practice of both *kata* and *kumite* by gradually integrating *kihon waza*. Students' introduction to *kumite* must begin simply and slowly so that they will not be overwhelmed at first. The objective is to preclude any sense of intimidation through perceived aggression; otherwise, beginners will find it difficult to trust either the control of their partners or the effectiveness of their own technique.

Maai

Practicing *kumite* introduces a student to the importance of *maai* (distance) for the first time. Knowing and trusting the space between oneself and one's partner enables the application of good, strong technique. Recognizing *maai* also builds confidence, allowing a *karate-ka* to determine what is a safe distance for and/or from attack.

Personal *maai* has always been present in the subconscious mind. At social gatherings one knows instantly if someone else is too close for comfort. If someone of the same sex stands too near, this might signal aggression. However, if someone of the opposite sex comes closer than usual, this could indicate signs of interest.

Kumite helps the student recognize, analyze and utilize *maai* for correct technical application. Obviously, the further away someone is, the safer one is going to feel, but increasing distance is not always a practical or viable alternative. A

David Tsuruoka demonstrates the use of maai.

karate-ka should use *maai* to first identify any sign of attack, and then to prepare for the correct course of action.

Although many variables dictate *maai*, techniques are generally launched from three basic distances. The first is long range, approximately two full steps away from an opponent. This range is used to determine an opponent's style, manner and intent. International karate competitions usually begin with this *maai* as opponents try to analyze each other's posture, tactics and timing. Techniques initiated from this distance are long, deep and powerful, sometimes requiring a step forward before they are launched. Long side thrust kicks, linear lunge punches and combination attacks are prevalent.

Mike Spence maintains composure by practicing maai concepts as the attack is initiated.

The second and most commonly practiced *maai* is medium range, in which a *karate-ka* assumes a stance one to one-and-a-half full steps from an opponent. Techniques thrown from this distance must be quick and powerful, and should achieve maximum extension. This range is most often used in national competition and in *dojo* training. *Karate-ka* are often seen shifting stances forward and back to gain control in these situations. Straight reverse punches and jabs, takedowns, foot sweeps, and front and roundhouse kicks would be some of the techniques initiated here.

The third distance is close range, usually no more than half a step away from an opponent. Stances here are short, compact and strong. Circular techniques are common, for example, hook punches, open-hand strikes, and *gedan mawashi-geri* to the knees and thighs. Close, quick takedowns and elbow and knee strikes can be very effective at this *maai*. This distance is utilized most when a *karate-ka* is cornered or there is limited space to maneuver, seen most commonly in crowded *dojo* training or in cramped street-defense scenarios.

Top and Bottom:
In this series O-Sensei explains takedown concepts to a Wednesday night black belt class.

Overleaf: *David Tsuruoka explores close fighting techniques.*

Categories of Kumite

6

組み手の部類

Gohon- and Sanbon-Kumite

When *karate-ka* first begin to interact with partners on the *dojo* floor, the instructor's first objective is to leave students with a positive experience and a desire to learn more. A powerful *mae-geri* thrown at a beginner by an advanced student would not only preclude a suitable response at the time but would also seriously inhibit subsequent performance for quite some time afterwards.

To prevent this from happening, a beginner is initially taught *gohon-kumite* (five-step sparring), either against someone of the same grade or someone of higher rank who appreciates a beginner's state of mind. This familiarizes a student with various attacks by giving him/her five chances to block a technique before a defending counter is expected (usually a reverse punch).

At this level, interaction is very formal and all moves are prearranged. Formalities - bowing, announcing intent, setting in stances, etc. - promote awareness, courtesy and respect. The use of only prearranged moves means that students need not be concerned about any surprises, fakes or sneak attacks. This in turn prevents them from developing bad habits such as twitches, overexertion, poor posture, etc. The instructor knows exactly which techniques will be thrown and so can watch closely for errors. If a student can concentrate on a single set of predetermined techniques, he/she will be able to work on speed, *kime* and *zanshin* with no distractions. Achieving a strike on

Students practice controlling techniques

target or blocking every technique is not the goal at this level. Instead, students should let the ego subside and work on poise, timing, posture, spirit and *maai*.

The path of *gohon-kumite* is linear - all attacks are thrown by stepping in a straight line toward the defender. The defender steps back and blocks the five attacks, throws a counter technique and holds strong *zanshin* at full extension of the counter for three seconds. The two partners then stand up into *heiko-dachi* (parallel ready stance) - the defender steps back and the attacker steps up towards the defender. Partners should never stand up in the direction of the attacker - this would imply aggression and a poor attitude by the defender.

Sanbon-kumite (three-step sparring) is almost identical to *gohon-kumite* except that the number of attacks is reduced to three. This forces defenders to prepare for a counter sooner than had been previously practiced. At the same time, attackers now only have three chances to penetrate their partners' defenses, obliging them to apply themselves even more diligently.

Sanbon-kumite is usually introduced fairly early in training (around fifth *kyu*). Many schools - especially those in cities - bypass *gohon-kumite* and teach *sanbon-kumite* right from the beginning due to limited floor space. This is acceptable as long as *sanbon-kumite* is still introduced with the same care and detail a novice would receive in *gohon-kumite*.

Although *sanbon-kumite* is one of the earliest forms of sparring taught, it should be practiced throughout the career of any serious *karate-ka*. New *kumite* principles can be applied to keep three-step sparring relevant and interesting. The concepts of *tai-sabaki* (evasive side stepping) can be introduced to intermediate *karate-ka* during the counterattack phase. This adds a new dimension: prior to this point, all attacking and defending movements will have been linear, as if a confrontation were taking place down a narrow alley. The defender now has the option of stepping in a multitude of directions to avoid a strike.

When first learning the principles of *tai-sabaki*, *karate-ka* must be careful not to become too ambitious with techniques or stances. Instead, they should remain focused and disciplined, striving to maintain sure-footed balance and stable posture. Confidence in *tai-sabaki* opens the door to learning the advanced timing principles of *sen-no-sen* and *sen* (see Chapter 7). A good foundation in basic *tai-sabaki* principles also helps the development of strong takedown techniques at the advanced level.

Kihon Ippon-Kumite

Kihon ippon-kumite (basic one-step sparring) is usually introduced at the intermediate level (around second *kyu*). It is the perfect balance point between *kihon waza* and *kumite*. All the formalities of establishing intent beforehand are present, as in *gohon-* and *sanbon-kumite*, but the exchange is now reduced to

Tom Pryde counters an attack with a side thrust kick.

O-Sensei practicing kumite with his students

only one attack. This results in a stronger emphasis on intensity and *zanshin* which makes a world of difference for the novice or intermediate *karate-ka* - it is the key psychological element that begins to transform *karate-do* from a mere exercise form into a real art of self-defense.

The defender realizes the person standing in front of him/her will have a single chance to strike. The attacker has presented him/herself with all the correct formalities: the technique and its intended location have been stated. Polite respect has been exchanged to acknowledge honor between equals. The attacker adopts a long ready stance while the defender remains in *heiko-dachi* - both with strong *zanshin*. The attack is launched with speed and controlled ferocity. If the attack is not blocked, contact could be made and injury could possibly result.

Prearranged sparring is the only time where contact with a partner would be tolerated, and only in the case of the attacker.

Top and Bottom: *In this series Tsuruoka Sensei controls an attack from Leo Cossetto, then counters with a powerful reverse punch to the solar plexus.*

If the defender were struck, it would not be because the attacker were malicious in any way, but because the defender was not properly prepared for the exchange. Contact would thus be the responsibility of the defender.

If a defender were struck and he/she retaliated by making contact on the counter, this would be considered a loss of control and an indication of poor character. In addition to committing a serious breach of etiquette, the defender would risk injuring a now-defenseless partner. Once an attack has been completed, the attacker may not continue movement in any way, for example, by blocking or avoiding the defending counter. He/she must remain motionless with strong *kime* and *zanshin* until the exchange has been completed. While this practice might appear a bit harsh to some outsiders, instances of contact are actually quite rare, thanks to the strict rules and formalities that every *karate-ka* must observe.

This factor of "attacking intent" begins to alter the mental state of a *karate-ka*, adding a new dimension to the purpose of training and to the meaning of *karate-do* itself. The psychological feeling of withstanding aggression helps a student develop the *budo* spirit which is the nucleus of any Asian martial art.

Tsuruoka *Kihon Kumite*

After acquiring some understanding of basic sparring principles, Tsuruoka *karate-ka* are introduced to another method of exchange developed from *ippon-kumite*. All rules, formalities and principles remain as before; the difference occurs at the point where the defender counters the initial attack. Rather than having both partners come up to attention to prepare for the next attack, the exchange is allowed to continue with the defender and attacker switching roles. The original attacker is now permitted to block the original counter technique and initiate a defensive counter of his/her own. This second counter technique is then blocked and countered, and a continuing cycle of attack and defense develops.

Tsuruoka *kihon kumite* is an excellent means of introducing the concepts of *tai-sabaki*: students discover the need to evade and counter partners' techniques by means other than stepping directly backwards. This system of exchange successfully demonstrates the relationship between *kata bunkai* and the timing and responses required in *kumite*.

Jiyu-Ippon Kumite

If karate applications were defined by a number scale with *kihon waza* at 0 and *jiyu-kumite* at 10, one would see a gradual, positive shift as *karate-ka* advance in skill. *Gohon-kumite* would sit at 2, *sanbon-kumite* at 3 or 4 and *ippon kumite* at 5. *Jiyu-ippon kumite* (free one-step sparring) would sit closest to free sparring at 8.

Jjiyu-ippon kumite removes a small portion of the protective formalities found in the previous levels of sparring discussed above. Students must still bow to each other and announce intent, but timing information and preparatory movements are no longer communicated. At this stage *karate-ka* are allowed greater freedom of personal expression, as the years spent on disciplined formalities can be trusted to keep exchanges under control and free from heightened egos.

In keeping with earlier *kumite* rules, a *karate-ka* first learning the principles of *jiyu-ippon kumite* still needs to call out the technique that will be launched. The difference with *jiyu-ippon kumite* appears in the actions which follow once the technique has been called. The attacker is now given full freedom of movement: precise stepping and formal stances are now replaced by shifting, stepping, slight hip fakes and different timing rhythms. The defender is also allowed to move around to prepare for the attack, still knowing which technique is coming and where it is intended to impact.

As timing improves and confidence grows, *karate-ka* can be brought one step closer to pure *jiyu-kumite* by eliminating one more formality. Once set in *kumite-dachi,* the attacker no longer announces the technique, only the level of the attack: *jodan, chudan* or *gedan* (high, middle or low). Now the defender must be keenly alert during the exchange while ensuring that his/her composure does not falter.

One factor that must remain constant throughout the beginning and advanced stages of *jiyu-ippon kumite* is the moment just after the exchange of techniques has been completed. It is still crucial for the attacker to remain motionless and solid in stance once the technique has been properly completed, i.e., there must be no secondary motion that could throw off *kime* and *zanshin*. Thrusts or punches must remain at full extension by utilizing pressure, compression and extension (see Chapter 3). Whipping strikes, such as *uraken*, must snap back tightly and remain focused; kicks must be completed with strong retraction followed by a strong definitive stance. The defender must be precise and focused with the counter technique. *Messen* is paramount: if both attacker and defender work together as one unit, there should not be any need for verbal communication. Both partners will know when the exchange has finished and will return to the ready position in unison.

Jiyu-Kumite and *Sport-Kumite*

Jjiyu-kumite is the final stage of *kumite* development. The purpose at this level is to explore pure timing and the freedom of personal expression. It must not be seen as a system of defense - the technical theories of *jiyu-kumite* do not coincide with the objective for which karate was originally developed, i.e., self-preservation in deadly combat. Techniques were originally designed to penetrate armor and continue on into the warrior behind it, but this kind of application is clearly no longer appropriate for *dojo* practice or sporting competitions. Today's *karate-ka* thus learn to adjust the extension of techniques to prevent injury, a practice known as *sun-dome*. This involves stopping a technique just short of the intended target, sometimes as close as just touching the opponent's skin.

As stated previously, ego friction between partners must be left out of *kumite*. There should be no feelings of uncontrolled aggression, only concentration on the exchange itself.

Sport-kumite match in Toronto.

Complete mutual respect must be evident. If any contact were to be made, it should be purely by accident, cause very little injury and be immediately forgiven with no malicious intent to "get even" whatsoever.

The extreme difficulty at this stage of *kumite* is in applying *kime* to all techniques. *Kime* is the one factor that distinguishes *jiyu-kumite* from self-defense: it is withheld to a large extent in the former but would be projected at full force in the latter. The reduction or absence of *kime* application is also one of the factors used to define noncontact sport/tournament karate. Techniques in sport karate usually involve linear whipping actions, thrown at maximum speed but void of power. This type of application helps prevent injuries while still allowing *karate-ka* to explore timing concepts.

One theory given for the introduction of sport karate is that it was developed to train students to handle adrenaline surges in intimidating situations. Another is that it was a recreational diversion from the everyday rigors of hard *dojo* training. Whatever its origins, sport karate offers an excellent means of developing timing under mentally trying conditions.

The aim is to psychologically condition a *karate-ka* to control the stress he/she would undoubtedly feel in an actually threatening encounter.

To summarize the difference between sport karate and traditional *karate-do*, the former is a kind of game, a recreational diversion whose purpose is to develop timing, strategy and composure. Techniques are of secondary importance and are designed to touch and retract from a specified target in order to gain points and determine a winner. The latter also develops excellent timing, but techniques and targets are geared more toward self-defense or "street applications." Mental discipline is much more focused than in sport karate and there is no concept of victor and vanquished, only equals working together to learn effectively.

Sport-kumite match in Toronto.

In these 4 photos David Tsuruoka practices kumite with Martin Hung and John Charry. Note the loose hands used in the exchange. This exercise practices timing, speed and foot work. Keeping the hands loose prevents injury and keeps the practitioners relaxed and fluid.

Principles of Timing

7
タイミングの原則

Once *karate-ka* begin to understand the purpose for which sparring was developed, *kumite* almost takes on a life of its own, seemingly void of any participants. Stances and energy levels adjust automatically, speed and power are naturally generated and techniques begin to flow effortlessly. This sense of autonomic response is actually inherent in everyone: if an animal snaps out, one jumps back, if lightning strikes, one seeks shelter, if a baby cries, one tries to comfort it. *Kumite* enables *karate-ka* to access this type of response through continuous training in different timing principles. These have been placed into three main categories of interaction over many years of research and practice by past *karate-do* masters. Each category is based on a number of factors such as personal aggression level, physical stature, technical ability, terrain and perception of intent.

O-Sensei demonstrates a counter technique.

Go-no-Sen

Go-no-sen is the first interactive timing category. Presented to the novice but developed through a lifetime of training, it is basically defined as "taking the initiative later." When a technique is thrown at a defender, he/she focuses intent on blocking or avoiding contact. Once the attack has been suppressed, a strong counter is used to overpower the attacker.

Go-no-sen could be interpreted as the most secure response to an attack. It offers the strongest defense as protection of the defender is the primary strategic objective. For practical application, *go-no-sen* could be resorted to when a *karate-ka* finds him/herself alien to the surroundings (for example, a new building or a different part of town) and is unfamiliar with the intent or ability of an opponent (a bully on the street, or a martial artist from a different system).

Go-no-sen: block attack, then follow with counter strike.

Sen-no-Sen

Sen-no-sen is a more advanced form of interaction between attacker and defender. "Taking the initiative simultaneously" is the goal of *sen-no-sen*, and the timing of techniques is crucial for successful execution. The defender must watch for an opponent's strike with strong and continuous *zanshin*. As the attacker starts to move, the defender simultaneously throws a counter technique, often together with a block, to intercept and suppress the attack.

Sen-no-sen provides the opportunity to finish an aggressive action quickly while still allowing a blocking technique to protect the defender. For practical application, *sen-no-sen* is ideal for making a fast escape from harm's way. It would be employed when a *karate-ka* is alien to the surroundings (a parking lot, a different *dojo* or competition venue) but familiar with an opponent's intent (a mugger, or a fellow *karate-ka* in a tournament).

Sen-no-sen: Block and counter at the same time.

Sen: catching the opponent before the attack is complete.

Sen

Sen is the most technically difficult of the three interactive timing categories and requires years of disciplined training to master. While *sen* can be defined as "taking the initiative first," it should never be interpreted as an attacking concept. A *karate-ka* waits and watches very closely with strong *zanshin* for any physical or strategic indication of an attack coming. As soon as such an indication has been detected, a counter is thrown before the attacker's technique can reach full speed and power. Although difficult to master, this timing principle is the most effective. Not only does it preclude an attack from reaching the mark, it also disrupts strategic intent, sapping an opponent's will to attack.

To apply *sen* in *kumite*, a *karate-ka* must have complete confidence in his/her ability and timing. There is no room or time in *sen* to block an attack, which means if the defender's timing is off by even a fraction of a second the attacker could win the exchange. It is thus a high-risk encounter, but one which can yield optimum results.

For practical application, *sen* would be employed when a *karate-ka* is familiar with both the surroundings (one's own neighborhood, place of work or home *dojo*) and an opponent's intent (a hooligan or a *karate-ka* from the same *dojo*). Familiarity with both the environment and the opponent enhances detection of impending aggression and allows a defender to take the initiative as soon as the attacker projects intent.

In extreme situations, such as when an attacker is about to present a concealed weapon, the best response is always immediate and complete disengagement, i.e., withdrawing to safety as quickly as possible. Where this is not possible, however, the application of *sen* - if practiced and timed correctly - could mean the difference between life and death. An attacker with a weapon is not in his/her right mind and must be dealt with quickly according to circumstances.

Jon Juffs and John Walker from Newmarket, Ontario, practice jiyu-kumite.

This kind of extreme case is, of course, something which everyone should seek to avoid at all costs. No one should ever have to weigh the risks of acting preemptively (possibly facing an assault charge in court) against letting a threatening person take the initiative (fighting for one's life in a hospital). This is one of the paradoxes of *karate-do*: one trains as if one might have to use a technique one day but with the higher aim of never having to use it.

Sen thus takes a *karate-ka* to a whole new level of moral and spiritual awareness. On the one hand, constant training in technical *sen* applications increases a *karate-ka*'s confidence in his/her ability to handle any situation. On the other hand, it brings home in a direct and very personal way the devastating power of karate. This in turn should instill a strong sense of respect for others and a firm commitment never to use this power aggressively.

David Tsuruoka practicing sen-no-sen.

The Spirit of Karate-do

空手道の精神

8

The Karate *Dojo*

Karate-do is now practiced in almost every country in the world. A traveling *karate-ka* would soon discover many contrasts in *dojo* construction and locations. Hunting around Kagoshima, Japan, one could find a small tin-roofed structure with dirt floors and no walls that is home to a small, but devoted group of practitioners. Many *karate-ka* in the United Kingdom train in school gyms or church basements. Some German and other European karate organizations have enough funds to build beautiful, spacious facilities, gathering three hundred *karate-ka* at a time to practice. The Japan Karate Association (JKA) had its headquarters in a large refurbished bowling alley in Tokyo until its separation in 1991. Older industrial complexes seem popular around Toronto, Canada. Despite these geographical and physical differences, one always seems to encounter a certain sense of familiarity in any karate *dojo*.

Cleaning the floor after training has a spiritual as well as a sanitary purpose

Karate-ka begin to associate this sense of familiarity with the camaraderie and collective determination which develop among peers. This sense does not change even if the location of practice changes. On a hot summer day, training in the park with fellow *karate-ka* creates the same energy level as training on a familiar indoor floor. Those fortunate enough to be able to upgrade facilities and expand training space do not have to start over in developing that hidden sense again: it comes with the members.

What could explain the existence of this sense or spirit from location to location? Is it the *sensei* who leads the *dojo*? Not exactly - if the *sensei* is ever away, the feeling is still there driving the workouts while students wait for his/her return. And when *karate-ka* travel to different *dojo* they find the same sort of feeling is usually present pushing the members at each particular school, regardless of who is teaching. Even as students come and go over the years there does not seem to be any diffusion or dilution of this sense or spirit.

Contemplation of the above may suggest that the *sensei*, the *dojo* and the disciplined nature of practice all somehow contribute to the ubiquitous development of the *karate-do* spirit. The biggest factor, however, may well be the intense emotional commitment each individual makes to the art. It can be said: the heart will lead a *karate-ka* down the road of personal growth.

A Way of Life

It has been said that *karate-do* is a way of life. While this may be open to varying degrees of interpretation, a single unifying theme can be readily identified. Students who choose to train in a traditional martial system adopt a philosophy of constant discipline, self-discovery and cooperation with others - a "way" of being which enriches their lives personally, socially and spiritually. The commitment to finding a higher meaning through training can be seen in both past and present examples.

As the need for historically ruthless combat techniques diminished, most martial arts systems shifted emphasis from incapacitating an adversary (the taking of life) to the perfection of character (understanding life's lessons). As seen in Chapter 1, this change was symbolized by the adoption of the new suffix *do* (the "way").

The historical transition from *jutsu* to *do* finds a modern parallel in the relationship between the sport and *do* aspects of many martial arts today. Once a martial artist's sport career

Knuckle push-ups condition the hands and strengthen the spirit.

has ended - due to age, injury or other physical limitations - he/she must look for other sources of personal challenge and development. Many practitioners may turn to completely new and unrelated interests, but some will choose to explore the *do* of their art, seeking to understand and apply the discipline, philosophy, ethics and values encompassed in its teachings.

The concept of *do* presents itself as a road which everyone must travel. There are no short cuts along the way: each lesson must be experienced and each challenge met before a person moves on to the next level. Similar concepts can also be found in many Western teachings. Catholicism, for example, structures religious development as a journey in which adherents are guided at different life stages by the seven sacraments: baptism, confirmation, the Eucharist, matrimony, confession, ordination and extreme unction.

O-Sensei making his rounds on the dojo floor.

Secular equivalents can be found in educational and social development. Children establish a foundation of knowledge for determining absolutes - right from wrong, good from bad, etc. They subsequently grow and progress to an intermediate level of relative awareness, discovering personal talents and limitations along the way. They are then given the responsibility of determining the direction these talents will be applied, improved and displayed. A select few will advance from student to teacher or from follower to leader as their character develops to match their talents.

Once someone has identified a personal way in life, he/she comes to realize that there is no end to the efforts that must be put forth. *O-Sensei* observes that "we are all beginners and will always continue to learn."

We are beginners when we are born.

We are beginners when we go to school.

We are beginners when we leave our parents' home.

We are beginners when we marry.

We are beginners when we have children.

We are beginners when we retire.

We are beginners when we die.

Bowing before the kata can begin.

Once a karate-ka learns the basics as a kyu belt, his/her karate training can truely begin. Grading to black belt symbolizes that beginning, placing your life in the hands of your sensei.

O-Sensei preforming a jumping side kick in the mid 1960s.

The History of Tsuruoka Karate-do

鶴岡空手道

9

Masami Tsuruoka was born on January 12, 1929, in Cumberland, British Columbia. He lived there until the Second World War, when the government of Canada - the country of his birth - placed him and his family in internment camps for longer than he wishes to remember. The Tsuruoka family was relocated to a camp in Roseberry, B.C. for a few years and then to another camp in Tashmi, B.C. for another year.

The Tashmi school system offered many children the opportunity to practice a martial art. Young Masami chose judo over *kendo* due to his young age and the lack of available *kendo* equipment. Thus began his lifelong relationship with the Japanese martial arts.

Photo of O-Sensei, taken in the early 1960s.

In 1945 the Tsuruoka family separated. While his older brother and sister remained in Canada, Masami and his father moved to Kumamoto, a small Japanese town on the west coast of Kyushu. There he continued his schooling and judo practice. He had always loved the martial arts and he continued to excel in sports. He worked hard at judo under the direction of Masahiko Kimura *Sensei*, quickly receiving his black belt. Nevertheless, Masami often felt he was too light for judo and this had frustrated him.

One day, Masami made a trip to Tokyo to apply for his citizenship papers. While exploring the capital, he came across a karate demonstration which opened his eyes wide with enthusiasm and awe. People were moving with lightning speed, striking and kicking ferociously but with pinpoint accuracy. Masami felt his heart pounding as he watched; in that instant he knew the direction his martial training would take.

As he watched the *karate-ka*'s precise movements, a bitter memory returned of being jumped from behind and beaten by four thugs in a case of mistaken identity. Masami had been left wondering what good judo was to him anymore. How could judo defend against multiple attackers bent on smashing his face? This question was put to rest by the karate demonstration he was now seeing. The art that he had so far only heard about would henceforth become the driving force in his life. He now knew he had to find a karate *dojo* somewhere near Kumamoto and begin training immediately.

Masami began studying *karate-do* at the age of eighteen under Dr. Tsuyoshi Chitose, the founder of *chito-ryu* karate. He trained every day in secret - even his own family had no idea of his training schedule until one morning they awoke to a disturbing pounding noise.

As soon as he woke up every day Masami would strike the *makiwara* in private behind his home. As he grew stronger, the pounding became louder and his secret was eventually discovered by his family. His father was very upset at what he felt was a complete waste of time. "What would others think, Masami?" his father would shout, "Only *yakuza* (gangsters) and assassins practice karate!" Masami's loving wife, however, supported his interest and encouraged him to keep training. She even began training herself, becoming a very proficient *karate-ka* in her own right.

Years went by and Masami spent his days working for the American armed forces for income, following his hobby of

Dr. Chitose, the founder of chito-ryu karate-do.

baseball and deepening his love for and dedication to *karate-do*. His proficiency in karate gave him the reputation of being one of Dr. Chitose's greatest students. Witnesses have recounted many of Masami's feats, such as his ability to shatter a *makiwara* with a single punch.[1]

In 1957 Mr. Tsuruoka returned to Canada, settling with his wife in Toronto, Ontario, to begin a career and raise a family. He began working at two jobs concurrently to make ends meet. Becoming a machinist for a number of local manufacturers, he eventually received a promotion to engineer. At this time, he had no intention of teaching *karate-do* and kept very quiet about his training. In his spare time he would only help teach judo at a local gym.

One day, a gentleman by the name of Kurt Uwe found out

- through friends at the Japanese consulate - about Tsuruoka *Sensei's* other talents and asked him if he would teach karate. The reply was a stern "No." In fact, Tsuruoka *Sensei* denied even knowing the art. Every day for six months Mr. Uwe would ask Tsuruoka *Sensei* to teach karate and every day the answer was "No, I don't know karate." Finally, after still further persuasion, Tsuruoka *Sensei* was convinced to teach his first karate class at the local judo club. Mr. Uwe then went on to help Tsuruoka *Sensei* open a small karate *dojo* on the top floor of a bakery in the East End of Toronto. While intentions were good, the location was bad: no one knew or heard about the small *dojo*. This *dojo* unfortunately closed after no students had come in for two months straight.

Tsuruoka *Sensei* then decided to take a new approach: if the people were not coming to him, he would go to the people. At this time, karate was an art few people knew anything about - it was time for an introduction.

He went to Mac's Gym, a large bodybuilding establishment in Toronto, to discuss the possibility of starting up a karate class there. The owner of the gym, Mac Mia, said, "We're having a Mr. Wasaga Beach bodybuilding competition, why don't you come and give a demonstration?" The invitation was accepted, and Kurt Uwe came to the competition as an assistant. The two men got up on the stage and began demonstrating some karate techniques, along with feats of brick- and board-breaking, all with the aim of presenting "karate power" to the "big boys." When the demonstration was over, Mac went to the microphone and immediately announced to everyone, "This is the new instructor at our gym!"

Tsuruoka *Sensei* taught at Mac's for four months until financial conflicts came into the picture. Students began to think it was time for him to have his own proper *dojo*. The efforts of students such as Ned Page, Benny Allen and Doug Harder saw this intention become a reality. The first operational karate *dojo* in Canada was established in 1958, on top of a bowling alley at 1944 Queen Street East, Toronto.

Tsuruoka Sensei and William Dometrich pose for a photo in Chicago, 1963.

Over time, Tsuruoka *Sensei* began to take an interest in learning the concepts and theories presented in other traditional styles of *karate-do*. Of those he had studied, it was the *shotokan* system that began influencing his teachings more than others. Many Japanese university students from the *shotokan* system would come to train at his *dojo* in Toronto. In return, they would teach classes and demonstrate their *kata*. *O-Sensei* fondly remembers *karate-ka* such as a certain Mr. Yuichi Hasegawa, Mr. Takenori Ogawa, Mr. Hasunori Ono and many others from Waseda, Keio and Hosei Universities.

Tsuruoka *Sensei* liked what *shotokan* had to offer: *kata* were very basic and dynamic, unlike the *chito-ryu kata* which he thought were more difficult and complex in their timing. *Chito-ryu* is an Okinawan-based system and its intricate moves make it somewhat more difficult to teach to students in Western culture. *Shotokan* karate, on the other hand could be taught to anyone without difficulty.

Two students working at Tsuruoka Sensei's summer camp, 1970s.

Shotokan had become a well-organized, standardized system through the efforts of Masatoshi Nakayama, chief instructor of the Japan Karate Association and director of the Physical Education department of Takushoku University. Nakayama *Sensei* had worked hard to present the *shotokan kata* as exercises designed to provide maximum personal benefit to all who practiced them.

As a few more years went by and Tsuruoka *Sensei*'s reputation grew, more and more students came to him for instruction; *chito-ryu* was becoming strong in Canada thanks to his efforts. Finances were still a challenge - Tsuruoka *Sensei* would pay out of his own pocket for things such as travel, rent and

Tsuruoka Sensei with Mr. Tsutomu Ohshima, early 1960s. Mr. Ohshima studied directly under Gichin Funakoshi, and founded the 1st U.S.A. karate organization in 1956.

O-Sensei (right) discussing karate's finer points with Mr. Sugiyama (center) and Mr. Kugazaki (left) at the U.S.A. Chito-kai national tournament, 1973.

Tsuruoka Sensei (standing in black jacket) and Mr. Hidetaka Nishiyama (sitting at O-Sensei's right) at the Calgary Nationals 1983. Mr. Nishiyama is a direct student of Gichin Funakoshi. He is one of the world's top karate masters, a respected author and a pioneer of U.S.A. shotokan karate.

visits from Dr. Chitose - but things were going well overall.

Tsuruoka *Sensei* began sending some of his students to train in Japan in order to broaden their technical range and to maintain regular communication between Kumamoto and Toronto. Two students benefiting from this exchange were Mr. Shane Higashi and Mr. David Akutagawa, both top students who had worked hard to help Tsuruoka *Sensei* promote *chito-ryu karate-do* in Canada.

After some time, Dr. Chitose began receiving money on a regular basis from Tsuruoka *Sensei*. These payments were offered as organizational dues to support the *Chito-kai* and Dr. Chitose's family. One day he telephoned Tsuruoka *Sensei* and asked for a substantial donation towards the building of a new headquarters in Kumamoto. Without hesitation Tsuruoka *Sensei* sent his own money to Dr. Chitose to help get construction under way.

Some time later Tsuruoka *Sensei* flew to Japan to see the new *dojo*. Instead, he was met with bad news. Dr. Chitose's deal had fallen through and all the money had been lost. Nevertheless, Dr. Chitose began explaining to Tsuruoka *Sensei* his plans for a different location and a grander design. This is when relations between the two men began to come under strain.

Upon Tsuruoka *Sensei's* return to Canada, Mr. Higashi suggested collecting a fee from each student that could be sent to Japan to help with the second *Hombu Dojo* (headquarters) project. Tsuruoka *Sensei* did not feel right charging people for this cause and declined.

Mr. Higashi then came forward and informed Dr. Chitose that he and Mr. Akutagawa would be willing to raise the money for him. Dr. Chitose subsequently made the decision to promote Mr. Higashi to the head of the *Chito-kai* in Canada, in effect replacing Tsuruoka *Sensei*. Those in the karate community learned of the changeover from Mr. Higashi rather than from Dr. Chitose.

Tsuruoka *Sensei* himself did not learn of the decision until a student in Calgary brought him up to date. He immediately called Japan and asked Dr. Chitose for an explanation but was given none. He found he had no alternative but to accept the situation and decided to fully resign from the *Chito-kai* before the changeover was made official.

Finding himself on his own, Tsuruoka *Sensei* was able to teach and advance as he saw fit. He began receiving phone calls and letters from prominent karate leaders from major styles in Japan, all wanting him to represent them in Canada. He was not sure how he was expected to do this since he did not fully know their style. In Tsuruoka *Sensei*'s view, these teachers wanted him to be a political figurehead - they would send someone else from Japan to actually teach the physical movements.

Although grateful for the consideration, Tsuruoka *Sensei* declined the invitations. Kept independent by his strong beliefs - and in spite of the recent differences with Dr. Chitose - he would say, "I only have one *sensei* and I will live and die with only one." Political conflicts can never alter *budo* ethics in Tsuruoka *Sensei*'s eyes. This attitude worked

O-Sensei in a traditional kimono for Japanese New Year at the Hombu, 1993.

to further enhance his image as many *karate-ka* from different styles came to respect and promote his ideals.

After a period of complete independence, Tsuruoka *Sensei* felt it was time to apply his efforts in the direction of sport karate. He wanted to see how his work would stand up to the world of karate around him. Gone were the days when schools would challenge each other to fights - instead, Tsuruoka *Sensei* put together a team of five or six students and set out across America on a series of road trips in search of tournaments. His team would travel the four corners of the United States, from Washington to Los Angeles, to New York and Chicago. There were no Canadian competitions at this time and travel became arduous and expensive, yet notably rewarding. Tsuruoka *Sensei* was happy with the results he saw and at the same time made a lot of good friends.

All of these positive experiences prompted Tsuruoka *Sensei*

The late C. Forgione scores a reverse punch while O-Sensei looks on (in background) at the 1983 Calgary Nationals.

to set up his next great undertaking. In 1963 he staged the very first Canadian karate tournament at Varsity Stadium in Toronto. The tournament was a tremendous success: people from all over North America came to compete and perform both cultural and martial art demonstrations.

Tsuruoka *Sensei* also became a well-respected referee on the early American karate scene. He is noted for officiating famous bouts between competitors such as Chuck Norris and Joe Lewis. Bruce Lee also had brief contact with Tsuruoka *Sensei* during Ed Parker's International Karate Championships in Long Beach, California, in 1964. Through a casual meeting and some subsequent correspondence, Mr. Lee and Tsuruoka *Sensei* exchanged ideas on the acceptance of foreign teachings by North American society.

In 1964 Tsuruoka *Sensei* decided to present his concepts of a unified karate system to the rest of Canada. The United States, in his eyes, was beginning to further subdivide into newly commercialized styles that were pulling away from traditional Asian concepts and values. Concerned that Canada would not be far behind in this trend, he established the National Karate Association (NKA) with the help of Doreen Davis, Ted Peterson and Frank Hatashita.

The NKA was set up to unite all traditional karate styles under one governing body. Each independent style would be free to develop as its history, syllabus and ideals dictated, yet at the same time would have the support of a government-sanctioned organization to assist in national and global interaction. All styles concerned accepted and liked the NKA, and in 1970 the Canadian national team was ready to compete internationally.

The NKA had quickly grown into a strong cohesive organization, but things were about to change. In 1974 the world of sport karate divided into two strong camps, the World Union of *Karate-do* Organizations (WUKO) and the International Amateur Karate Federation (IAKF). The two sport-oriented bodies were at odds over which group should represent karate

O-Sensei as a corner referee at a 1973 Kentucky (U.S.A.) karate tournament.

at the Olympics, and were never able to reconcile their differences. This division began to cause problems for Tsuruoka *Sensei* and the NKA in their efforts to coordinate standards and events with other associations domestically and internationally. The early 1980s became especially difficult for Tsuruoka *Sensei* as political issues eventually prompted his resignation as the head of the NKA. A cause he had worked so hard to promote was no longer a significant part of his life.

"Hardships are a fact of life," says *O-Sensei* today. Yet through all of these trials he still considers himself to be a very lucky man in the world of karate, having learned early on not to let political influences dictate his actions. On an earlier trip back to Japan he received some valuable advice from Minoru Miyata *Sensei* - a possible successor to Funakoshi *Sensei* at the Japan Karate Association until Miyata's untimely death. Miyata *Sensei* said, "Tsuruoka, do not worry about style, just follow your beliefs to the best of your abilities."

Over the years *O-Sensei* has observed many styles and has worked hard to personally incorporate the best from what he has seen. His is still adamant that the karate he teaches is not any one style and feels he has taken karate back to its roots where styles were nonexistent. He admires what Jigoro Kano *Sensei* has done for judo, creating a unified system of global interaction without "style politics." With this thought, *O-Sensei* cautions that "Style could be the one factor to defeat karate."

O-Sensei helping a student focus on target.

Over the years *O-Sensei* has come to embrace the roots of an art which now defines his every action. Students and instructors half his present age find his limitless energy and drive difficult if not impossible to keep up with on the *dojo* floor, and his innate understanding of kinetics and physiology have taken him to a level of mastery that would be difficult to match in the world today.

Friendships with great teachers such as Hidetaka Nishiyama *Sensei* of the United States (*shotokan*), Tatsuo Suzuki *Sensei* of England (*wado-ryu*), Stan Schmidt *Sensei* of South Africa (*shotokan*) and Frank Hatashita *Sensei* of Canada (judo) have kept *O-Sensei's* concepts open to constant positive influence throughout his many years of study and teaching.

O-Sensei confides, "It has been a difficult yet very rewarding career." He loves instructing at his *dojo* in Toronto and traveling to seminars across North America, sharing himself and his art with enthusiastic people from all walks of life. He truly personifies the spirit of *karate-do*.

Tsuruoka Sensei and Suzuki Sensei (wado-ryu). Good friends get together at summer camp.

Sketches in Time

時のスケッチ

10

Very few people in Canada would have known anything about *karate-do* before *O-Sensei* established the country's first karate *dojo* in 1958. Over the years, however, a great number of people from coast to coast have learned and benefited from this art.

O-Sensei's contribution to this tremendous growth has been previously related in historical, technical and organizational terms. It is at the personal level, however, where *O-Sensei* continues to have the greatest impact: he has always been held in the highest regard for his strength of character, his dedication to his students and his skills as a charismatic communicator.

When asked for personal images of *O-Sensei*, students respond with a wide range of recollections and feelings. A couple of these reminiscences have been included here in the hopes that they will inform, inspire and perhaps even rekindle the "spark" which keeps all *karate-ka* moving down the path of self-discovery.

O-Sensei and David Tsuruoka observing a demonstration.

Moving a Mountain

It is the first weekend of August 1992. *Karate-ka* from all parts of Canada have gathered in the small mountain town of Banff, Alberta, for the seventh annual Western Tsuruoka Summer Camp.[1] Everyone has settled in at the local YWCA, exchanged greetings with old and new acquaintances and explored the streets of Banff for souvenirs and refreshments.

Everyone is in good spirits the evening before training starts, although there is still a subtle sense of apprehension in the air. Many *karate-ka* either have not seen *O-Sensei* since last year's camp or are about to learn from him for the first time. They wonder: What will he expect of us this time? Has my training over the past year been enough to meet his high standards? Will I be the unfortunate individual singled out to illustrate poor form?

The main street of Banff, Alberta. Morning workouts are in the park, just left of the bridge in this photo.

The personal questions continue until *O-Sensei* makes his rounds before retiring. He seems in good spirits and asks everyone for news of their families and about their trip to Banff. He shares a traditional drink of sake with the higher-ranking *sempai* (senior students). All appears normal, and everyone gets a good first night's sleep.

Alarms start ringing at 5:00 a.m. - no one dares be late for the "assembly whistle." *O-Sensei* opens with a short review of rules and expectations, and the morning run begins.

Three hours later *karate-ka* have gathered for breakfast and to compare notes on the morning training session. "Inspirational! *O-Sensei* was in top form as usual," says Tom, an out-of-province visitor. Everyone at Tom's table responds enthusiastically - all are looking forward to the next class.

Over at one of the *"sempai* tables" the mood, though positive, is more introspective. John is thinking about *O-Sensei's* tight-release principle. "Frank," he asks, "do you think people will be able to pick up on this method of training? I know I'm having a tough time with it." "Don't worry," Frank replies, "it's only the first day - everyone is working hard and enjoying the experience."

The first day ends well after seven hours of training in three sessions. Everyone prepares for dinner and begins to think about the next day with *O-Sensei*. For the next couple of days this steady routine continues. The training proves difficult at the

Frank Prystupa of Calgary, Alberta, demonstrates the Shotokan kata-Heian sandan.

higher altitude, but all continue to work hard and with good energy.

The last day of training arrives and everyone is still trying their best. However a few are beginning to sense a certain uneasiness in O-*Sensei* "Nothing to really worry about, he's been working hard, too, and must be a little tired," suggests a young brown belt.

More students are becoming aware of O-*Sensei*'s discomfort. They increase their efforts - trying to please - but the harder they work the more he frowns. No one speaks, but most are thinking: Is *O-Sensei* ever really satisfied? What do we have to do to please such a perfectionist? Perspiration beads down faces as the *kata Bassai-dai* (penetrate the fortress) is practiced over and over, each performance bringing an even deeper look of concern to O-*Sensei*'s face.

It is the second-last workout of the final day of camp and O-*Sensei* has finally had enough. He stops the class and storms to the middle of the training area. "You people are like robots! No feeling, no *kime*, no *zanshin*! Everything I have taught you the past few days is nowhere to be seen! I will have to show you myself!"

The class is silent - *O-Sensei* very rarely demonstrates techniques himself. He usually has students do this for him, correcting them as they go until their form is acceptable. This way, students can see that correct execution is actually attainable by someone like themselves.

O-Sensei makes sure the hips move first!

O-Sensei has decided to illustrate the application of the *Bassai-dai*. He looks carefully around the room, then calls out, "Cornelius!" The largest man in the class steps forward and approaches *O-Sensei* slowly.

Cornelius stands six feet and three inches tall and is 260 pounds of solid muscle. In addition to being an amateur rugby player he holds the rank of *nidan* in Tsuruoka karate. Although a friendly man, no one ever wants him for a partner during *kumite* for obvious reasons.

Banff, Alberta, Summer Camp, 1993.

Cornelius is now directly in front of O-*Sensei*. The difference in size between the two men is almost comical: a 145-pound man in his sixties faces a enormous man in his prime who uses tremendous strength in almost all his daily activities.

The atmosphere is tense as the two men confront each other. *O-Sensei* shouts out *"oi-zuki!"* Cornelius sets, then lunges forward with his attack. However, because of the respect and admiration he has for *O-Sensei* the attack is weak, slow and off target. Cornelius seems afraid to hit the teacher who has given him so much over the years.

At the end of the punch *O-Sensei* steps back with a hard look of contempt, slaps Cornelius hard on the chest and shouts "Punch harder!" This time, Cornelius sets low in his stance with a look of concentration on his face. Time slows as the two men stare at each other.

Cornelius explodes with a shattering *kiai*, sending all of his power at the shorter man in front of him. But *O-Sensei* has already stepped in to strike him on the chest. The impact is so loud that everyone is certain both men have been injured. Cornelius is sent flying backwards five or six feet, barely able to stay on his feet.

O-Sensei, however, remains motionless, stable and focused: perfect *sen-no-sen*. Cornelius regains his balance uninjured, but is red in the chest from the impact and red in the face from embarrassment. *O-Sensei* smiles, walks over to the big man and puts his arm around him. "Tight-release," he says quietly as he proceeds to conclude the class.

A Leap of Faith

The energy in Trinidad is higher than usual today. The streets of Port of Spain are bustling with promoters, officials, competitors and spectators, all preparing for the big karate tournament which begins tomorrow morning. The year is 1972 and participants from all the Caribbean islands have come together to make this an event that will not be forgotten.[1]

Robert has been waiting for this day for months now. He has made sure that all his work at home has been completed. He has explained to his family the importance of this very special "karate day" so that he will not be required to complete any more chores.

Robert has a hard time sleeping the night before, even though he is not competing. He has only been training for a few years and is not quite ready to compete in a tournament this big. He loves karate so much, however, that just the thought of being in the stands gives him a rush of adrenaline.

At 7:00 a.m. there a knock at the door. It is Mark, one of Robert's training partners and a close friend. Mark has managed to get the day off work to go with Robert to the tournament. "We have to get there early and get a good seat!" says Mark. "This is like the Olympics, everyone will be there." They pack up a few things to eat and go to the front of Queen's Hall, the tournament venue. It may be a long wait but they will be sure to get a good seat.

At 10:00 a.m. the doors finally open. The two friends dash up the central stairway to the best seats they can find. The complex fills up quickly and is electric with anticipation. Anyone involved with *karate-do* is feeling especially excited, not just because of the strong competition expected, but

Preparing for the Tournament.

because Tsuruoka *Sensei* has apparently arrived from Canada and will be performing a demonstration during intermission. Tsuruoka *Sensei* is the chief *karate-do* instructor at the time not only for Canada, but also for all the Caribbean islands. He has gained a strong reputation as a gifted technician and a brilliant teacher in both regions.

Robert has only seen Tsuruoka *Sensei* a few times before at clinics. Unfortunately, Robert's lower rank has always put him at the back of the training floor, so he has never really had a clear view of what Tsuruoka *Sensei* has been doing. But this time, he has a central seat with no one in front of him, and Tsuruoka *Sensei* will not only be only teaching - Robert and Mark are sure he will provide a spectacular demonstration.

The competitors are fierce and energetic, *kata* performances are powerful and dynamic, and *kumite* is fast and strong, but controlled. It has been a great tournament so far. At intermission, the lights go dim except for the ones directly over the center of the complex.

The crowd becomes silent for the first time today - everyone is looking around to see which doorway Tsuruoka *Sensei* will enter through. A minute goes by. Then quietly, a short yet dynamic man walks to the center of the ring with Tony Paris following behind. A strong, stocky man, Tony is known by everyone as the head of *karate-do* in Trinidad and one of Tsuruoka *Sensei*'s students.

O-Sensei helping students with their basics.

With no verbal introduction the two men bow to each other. Tony begins throwing punches and kicks as Tsuruoka *Sensei* begins demonstrating *tai-sabaki* and strong counter techniques with perfect timing.

After five or six attacks, Tony comes in with *oi-zuki*. Tsuruoka *Sensei* lets out a shattering *kiai*, which causes most in the audience to jump. He darts toward Tony and in one motion blocks the technique, steps on Tony's front thigh and vaults over his head. He lands directly behind Tony in a perfectly balanced stance with one arm stretched straight up.

Everyone, including Tony, is shocked by this display of speed and timing. Robert and Mark look at each other wondering what has actually happened. Tony is still standing - there is no visible sign of any counter technique having been performed.

Feeling a cool breeze on his back, Tony is the first to realize what has transpired. He turns to show the audience. The complex erupts with applause. Tony's heavyweight *karate-gi* (training uniform) has been perfectly split from the base of the neck to the belt around his waist. While jumping over Tony's head, Tsuruoka *Sensei* had brought the first two fingers of his outstretched hand down on the top of Tony's *karate-gi*.

Robert and Mark are speechless. Others in the audience are murmuring about the spectacle they have just witnessed. As the two men walk toward the changeroom and the tournament continues, Tsuruoka *Sensei* whispers to Tony, "I will buy you a new *karate-gi*."

O-Sensei preforming one of the fantastic feats he is known for (early 1960s). His jumping kicks could reach heights of 5-6 feet.

Words of Encouragement

激励の言葉 11

The following are notes and comments written down by *O-Sensei* over the years. He has assembled these in the hope they will help *karate-ka* work through both training questions in the *dojo* and larger issues on the journey through life. Small points with a strong message, they are meant for students at all levels to contemplate and enjoy.

Mokuso - At the beginning of class, students must use meditation to clear the mind in order to observe and see clearly the objective and teaching of the *sensei* (much like emptying a cup).
Hansei - At the end of class, students must meditate and review the teachings from the *sensei* while their minds are still focused. Each student must clearly see the teachings in his/her mind.
Effort - Practice makes perfect. Persistent practice leads to real ability and produces the perfect result. With persistent outward action (physical), you will achieve the concealed inner action, action without mind
Kihon - Without solid basic techniques you cannot perform *kata* nor do *kumite*. This is like learning the ABCs: without the

David Tsuruoka and Martin Hung demonstrate simultaneous high round house kicks.

full knowledge of letters you cannot form words or sentences to express meaning.

Time - Time is activity and action. Practice towards a goal without setting time limits. Eliminate deadlines to achieve a goal, for only frustration arises when your goal is not achieved "on schedule."

Discomfort - Pain while practicing is temporary, death is permanent.

Rest - Resting while in practice is not acceptable for you can rest forever on your deathbed.

Ego - Ego is everyone's downfall.

Self-control - Etiquette, self-control, patience. Always.

Attitude - A *karate-ka* must always honor his/her parents, be diligent in attendance and have respect for duly constituted authority. He/she must be willing to learn from everything.

Honesty and Sincerity - Trickery, cheating, deception and lying are not the answers to your success. Try to perform at the best of your ability; only then are you fully satisfied with your accomplishments.

Sport Karate - To compete is to test your skill against others. Winning is not the essence, the purpose is to expose the weaknesses or faults in your own techniques.

Some Remarks for Aspiring *Sensei*

- There are many *dojo* and instructors but very few *sensei*.
- When you come to the point where you think you know it all, compare yourself with a true master. This is when you realize how little you know.
- Instruct with action rather than talk.
- When you instruct beginners, be one with them. Work and learn with them. Only then will you understand the complexity of the art of karate.

Tsuruoka students posing in 3 basic shotokan stances.

- Analyze the individual and learn with him/her. Understand his/her age, degree of flexibility and physical ability. Then offer your wisdom with compassion and patience. Guide your student with self-assurance, spiritual inspiration and self-enlightenment.

Passion must be present in every endeavor, for without passion it is a useless venture. Wherever you find yourself practicing, working or teaching, do so with passion for people will feel it in you.

Guide Students with the Seven Senses:

- **TOUCH**
(not hit) - Work with partners, no need to smash to prove oneself.
- **HEARING**
(to listen) - Everyone can hear, only a few can listen.
- **SMELL**
Remember the old saying, "like rotten egg." Each emotion has a scent.
- **SEEING**
(not just looking) - Really see what is in front of you.
- **TASTE**
Know what is good or bad, do not follow blindly.
- **COMMON SENSE**
You know it, use it.
- **NON SENSE**
(fool, joker, clown) - Control your character.

NOTES

Chapter 1

1. Randall G. Hassell, *The Karate Experience: A Way of Life* (Rutland, Vermont: Charles E. Tuttle, 1980), p. 14.

2. Bruce A. Haines, *Karate's History and Traditions* (Rutland Vermont and Tokyo Japan: Charles E. Tuttle, 1995), p. 85.

Chapter 2

1. Jim LePlante of the science department at M. McGiveny High School in Markham, Ontario, states that centripetal force is the correct term for the effect created as objects move away from a central axis. Centrifugal force is a misnomer that has been popularized by the invention of the "centrifuge" used in science and medicine to separate liquids.

2. Based on data from a case study presented to the author at the University of Western Ontario Teacher's College (London, Ontario) during his Technological Studies program, 1992-93.

Chapter 4

1. Heino Engel, *Measure and Construction of the Japanese House* (Rutland, Vermont: Charles E. Tuttle Company, 1985), p. 20.

Chapter 5

1. Masatoshi Nakayama, *Best Karate, Volume 8: Gankaku, Jion* (Tokyo: Kodansha International, 1981), p. 12.

2. John Corcoran and Emil Farkas, *Martial Arts: Traditions, History, People* (New York: Gallery Books, 1993), p. 396.

Chapter 9

1. A Tsuruoka *karate-ka* in Toronto, Mr. Robin Gobin, has actually seen Tsuruoka *Sensei* split a makiwara with one blow. While Mr. Gobin was not in Kyushu when Tsuruoka *Sensei* was training with Dr. Chitose, he has heard similar accounts from senior acquaintances and students of Tsuruoka *Sensei*.

Chapter 10

1. The following is an eyewitness account by the author who attended the Western Tsuruoka Summer Camp in 1992.

2. The following is based on an eyewitness account by Mr. Robin Gobin, who was a member of the audience in Trinidad at the time.

GLOSSARY

AIKIDO	a modern, non-aggressive Japanese martial art which uses an opponent's momentum to apply locks or throws.
AIKIDO-KA	*aikido* practitioner(s)
ATE-WAZA	striking technique(s)
ATEMI	strike(s) to a specific part of the body
BASSAI-DAI	a *shotokan kata* which uses quick intercepting techniques and many changes of direction
BOGU	protective body armor worn in *kendo* and some full-contact karate styles
BUDO	the way of the warrior - (modern) martial way(s)
BUJUTSU	(older) martial fighting art(s)
BUNKAI	breakdown and practical interpretation(s) of *kata* techniques
CAPOEIRA	a Brazilian martial art which uses acrobatic skills to confuse and defeat an opponent, historically "hidden" in a dance
CH'UAN FA	Chinese unarmed fighting arts (Japanese: *kempo*)
CHITO-KAI	the governing association for *chito-ryu* karate, based in Kumamoto, Japan
CHITO-RYU	style of karate developed by Dr. Tsuyoshi Chitose (Dr. Chitose is known as Chinen Gua in Okinawa)
CHUDAN	middle level
DACHI	stance(s) (suffix form of *tachi*)
DAN	"stage/level" - black belt rank(s) (increasing in numerical order as a student advances)
DO	a suffix adopted by modern martial arts to imply a focus on character development (Chinese: *tao*)
DOJO	martial arts training hall
EMPI	a *shotokan kata* which uses quick movements in a variety of direction changes
GEDAN	low level
GEDAN-BARAI	low block
GERI	kick (suffix form of *keri*)
GO-NO-SEN	countering an attack after an opponent has launched it

GOHON-KUMITE	five-step sparring (prearranged)
GOJU-RYU	a "hard-soft" style of karate
GYAKU	reverse
GYAKU-ZUKI	reverse punch
HANSEI	reflection, introspection
HEIAN-SHODAN	the first *heian* (tranquillity) *kata,* presently taught to beginners in *shotokan* karate
HEIKO-DACHI	parallel stance (upright ready position with feet at shoulder width)
HIKITE	pulling hand
HOMBU	headquarters
IAIDO	the way of sword-drawing (modern) [older sword-drawing arts: *iai-jutsu*]
IBUKI	breathing
IKKEN-HISSATSU	ending a conflict with one deadly strike
IPPON	*kumite*: one-step sparring
JIYU-IPPON	*kumite*: free one-step sparring
JIYU -KUMITE	free sparring
JODAN	upper, high level
JUDO	modern martial art using throws and sweeps (Olympic sport)
JUJUTSU	a traditional grappling art which uses locks, throws and takedowns
JUTSU	"art/technique" - historical suffix signifying a martial art's emphasis on actual combat effectiveness
KARATE-DO	the way of the empty hand
KARATE-GI	karate training uniform
KARATE-KA	karate student(s)/practitioner(s)
KATANA	sword(s)
KATA	prearranged form(s) of set movements and techniques
KENDO	the way of the sword - modern Japanese fencing (historical form: *kenjutsu*)
KENDO-KA	*kendo* practitioner(s)
KERI	(*-geri*) kick
KERI WAZA	kicking technique(s)
KI	energy (Chinese: CH'I)

KIAI	a sharp cry emitted at the point of impact to increase focus and penetration
KIBA DACHI	horse-riding (straddle) stance
KIHON	basic(s)
KIHON DACHI	basic stance(s)
KIHON IPPON-KUMITE	basic one-step sparring (prearranged)
KIHON-WAZA	basic technique(s)
KIME	decisive focus
KIZAMI-ZUKI	jab
KOBUDO	way(s) of fighting with farm implements
KOEI-KAN	a Japanese karate system which uses protective body armor for full-contact sparring
KOKUTSU-DACHI	back stance
KUMITE	sparring
KUMITE-DACHI	sparring stance(s)
KYU	junior and intermediate grades (decreasing numerical order as a student advances)
MAAI	(*mawai*) interval or distance between sparring protagonists
MAE-GERI	front kick
MAKIWARA	wooden post with a straw or rubber pad at solar-plexus height, used to practice striking
MAWASHI-GERI	roundhouse kick
MESSEN	eye direction
MOKUSO	meditation, contemplation
NAGINATA	halberd(s)
N*IDAN*	second stage/level
OI-ZUKI	lunge punch
O-SENSEI	Great Teacher (honorific)
SANBON-KUMITE	three-step sparring (prearranged)
SEMPAI	a senior person in a Japanese hierarchical system (junior person: *kohai*)
SEN	preempting an attack as soon as it is detected and before it can occur
SEN-NO-SEN	countering an attack at the same time it is launched
SENSEI	teacher (respectful connotation)

SHITO-RYU	style of karate developed by Kenwa Mabuni which blends elements from both Naha-*te* and Shuri-*te* (see *shorei* and *shorin*)
SHODAN	first stage/level
SHOREI	(Naha-*te*) style of karate developed in the Okinawan city of Naha which tends to focus on strength and power
SHORIN	(Shuri-*te*) style of karate developed in the Okinawan capital of Shuri which tends to focus on speed and quickness
SHOTOKAN	the style of traditional karate taught by Gichin Funakoshi
SOTO-UKE	outside-in block
SUKI	a gap or lapse in concentration while facing an opponent
SUN-DOME	stopping a technique about one inch short of the target to avoid injuring one's partner
TACHI	(-*dachi*) stance(s)
TAI-SABAKI	evasive body movement (sidestepping)
TANDEN	abdominal focal point in meditation and all martial arts
TODE	"China hand" - a historical name for the Okinawan precursor to karate
TEKKI-SHODAN	a *shotokan kata* which uses powerful thrusting techniques supported by a solid low stance (*kiba-dachi*)
TAO	Chinese philosophical concept for the underlying principle or "way" of the universe and everything in it (Japanese: *do*)
TE	"hand" - a historical name for the Okinawan precursor to karate
TSUKI	(-*zuki*) punch(es), thrust(s)
UCHI-UKE	inside-out block
UKE	block(s), to receive
UKE-WAZA	blocking technique(s)
URAKEN	backfist
WADO-RYU	a style of karate known for powerful snapping techniques
WAZA	technique(s)
YANG	masculine principle in Chinese philosophy

YIN	feminine principle in Chinese philosophy
YOKO-GERI-KEKOMI	side thrust kick
ZANSHIN	a state of calm awareness and unwavering concentration
ZENKUTSU-DACHI	front stance
ZUKI	punch, thrust (suffix form of *tsuki*)

BIBLIOGRAPHY

Abele, Ridgely. Focus-Focus-Focus-Karate Profiles Made in America. Hamilton, Ohio: Holly Witherspoon Keys, January, February 1996.

Corcoran, John, and Emil Farkas. *Martial Arts: Traditions, History, People*. New York: Gallery Books, 1993.

Engel, Heino. *Measure and Construction of The Japanese House*. Rutland, Vermont: Charles E. Tuttle, 1985.

Haines, Bruce A. *Karate's History and Traditions*. Rutland, Vermont: Charles E. Tuttle, 1995.

Hassell, Randall G. *The Karate Experience: A Way of Life*. Rutland, Vermont: Charles E. Tuttle, 1990.

McCarthy, Patrick. *The Bible of Karate: Bubishi*. Rutland, Vermont: Charles E. Tuttle, 1995.

Nakayama, Masatoshi. *Best Karate, Volume 8: Gankaku, Jion*. Tokyo: *Kodansha* International, 1981.

Ratti, Oscar, and Adele Westbrook. *Secrets of The Samurai*. Rutland, Vermont: Charles E. Tuttle, 1973.

Reid, Howard, and Michael Croucher. *The Way of The Warrior*. London: Century Publishing, 1983.

Tohei, Koichi. *Ki in Daily Life*. Tokyo: Ki No Kenkyukai H.Q., 1978.

Ueshiba, Kisshomaru. *The Spirit of Aikido*. Tokyo: Kodansha International, 1984.

Urban, Peter. *The Karate Dojo*. Rutland, Vermont: Charles E. Tuttle, 1967.

M Tsurnoka